Wild Flowers
of the High Weald

Wild Flowers

of the High Weald

CHRIS CLENNETT

Kew Publishing
Royal Botanic Gardens, Kew

First published in 2018 by the Royal Botanic Gardens, Kew, Richmond, Surrey, TW9 3AB, UK
www.kew.org

ISBN 978-1-84246-662-9

Distributed on behalf of the Royal Botanic Gardens, Kew in North America
by the University of Chicago Press, 1427 East 60th St, Chicago, IL 60637, USA.

British Library Cataloguing in Publication Data
A catalogue record for this book is available from the British Library.

Production management: Georgina Hills
Design and page layout: Christine Beard
Copy-editing: Sharon Whitehead
Proofreading: Matthew Seal

Printed in Great Britain by Bell & Bain

MIX
Paper from
responsible sources
FSC® C007785

For information or to purchase all Kew titles please visit shop.kew.org/kewbooksonline or email publishing@kew.org

Kew's mission is to be the global resource in plant and fungal knowledge, and the world's leading botanic garden.

Kew receives about a third of its running costs from Government through the Department for Environment, Food and Rural Affairs (Defra). All other funding needed to support Kew's vital work comes from members, foundations, donors and commercial activities, including book sales.

CONTENTS

INTRODUCTION

The High Weald is an Area of Outstanding Natural Beauty running across West Sussex, East Sussex and Kent. Within it many varied habitats can be found, from planted and tended gardens to lowland heath, meadows and woodlands. The wide range of habitats across the High Weald and the varied topography of this landscape mean that a huge number of wildflowers grow here naturally. Careful management of the gardens, woodlands, heathland and reserves is undertaken to conserve and increase the biodiversity in all of these areas. Within the Weald, the Wakehurst Millennium Seed Bank is home to a global conservation initiative, in which the seeds of both native and threatened exotic plants are saved for the future.

HISTORY OF THE HIGH WEALD LANDSCAPE

Sandwiched between the chalk hills of the North and South Downs is a region of sandstone cliffs and steep-sided valleys, known as 'ghylls'. This landscape is known as the High Weald. 'Weald' comes from the Old English 'wald' or 'wood', and thanks to its special characteristics this landscape has remained more densely forested than any other area of southern England.

The geology of the High Weald results from land folding as the Alps were formed. The chalk of the North and South Downs has been eroded to reveal underlying clay and sand layers and within them a dense sandstone layer. The Tunbridge Wells Sands lie beneath Grinstead Clay, but the region between East Grinstead, Tunbridge Wells and Crowborough, the dense sandstone rock referred to as Ardingly Sandstone, is now exposed in places to form cliffs and outcrops. This is the defining character of the High Weald, distinguishing it from the softer and richer clay soils of the Low Weald. The dramatic cliffs, ravines, gullies and ridges mean that the High Weald was unsuitable for large-scale clearance and agriculture, so it has not been settled in the same way as the surrounding land. Instead, the forest was managed to support the iron industry and as a feeding ground or 'pannage' for swine. Iron ore was plentiful and easily accessible through open cast mines. Iron was extracted by 'smelting', a process that required high-quality charcoal to produce sufficient heat. Even in prehistoric times, people were coppicing understorey trees such as hornbeam and hazel to produce a sustainable harvest of wood to make charcoal. The iron industry remained significant in the Roman era (several Roman roads run through the High Weald close to areas where iron working was centred) and saw a resurgence in medieval times (the remains of furnace or hammer ponds are frequent in the area and Britain's first blast furnace was located near Coleman's Hatch at

lowland heath and woodland
form a patchwork of habitats

the edge of Ashdown Forest). Indeed, the landscape of the High Weald is amongst the best-preserved medieval landscapes in Europe.

Although the High Weald was extensively wooded, it is important to remember that areas such as Ashdown Forest did not gain this name because they are forests in the current meaning of the word. Ashdown Forest was always a matrix of woodlands and open areas of heathland and grasses. An area of around 20 square miles was enclosed by a pale in Norman times to form a hunting forest. However, tenants of the land remained as 'commoners' who continued to graze their animals throughout the Forest, preventing the establishment of tree seedlings and retaining the open grassland. It remained a hunting forest for deer prior to the Civil War, when the deer were eradicated

sandstone outcrops

and the fence removed, but was then re-established as a deer park with the restoration of the monarchy. Part of the Forest was sold off in the late seventeenth century as a rabbit farm (hence the name 'warren' appears in several place names).

In several large estates, such as Wakehurst in the west of the High Weald, more recent alterations can be seen alongside the ancient features. Sandstone outcrops that naturally appear across the woodlands were modified in the nineteenth century to create picturesque walks and carriage drives. Extensive tree planting began in the early twentieth century,

ornamental ponds

transforming areas of open farmland into arboreta. Medieval fish ponds were converted into ornamental garden features including, at Wakehurst, the Water Gardens and Mansion Pond.

Changes of use within the gardens and woodlands have all altered biodiversity. At Wakehurst, Bloomers Valley was ploughed for potato growing during the Second World War, then converted to mown grass, before being transformed into a Wealden wildflower meadow. Similar changes across the entire estate have affected the array of wildflowers that are able to thrive, but during the 50 years of Kew's management, the aim has always been to enhance the estate while conserving the native wild plants.

Similarly, since their inception in 1885, the Conservators of Ashdown Forest have managed the land for the owners and commoners to enhance and restore the biodiversity of the habitats. Extensive scrub and bracken colonisation resulted from changes to the traditional farming of the Forest, threatening many of the rarest habitats. A programme of clearing scrub and scraping off the bracken layer to re-sow with heathers and grasses is helping to retain the best that the Forest offers.

RANGE OF HABITATS IN THE HIGH WEALD

The High Weald contains a wide variety of habitats, which are of extraordinary value in a part of Britain that is generally densely built on and within close proximity to London. To find semi-natural woodland, lowland heath, established wildflower meadows, rare remnant Atlantic coast flora, as well as well-maintained gardens and estates in public and private hands so close to the capital is an incredible thing. This makes the High Weald all the more valuable and an area to be treasured and explored. For this reason, the High Weald was designated an Area of Outstanding Natural Beauty (AONB) in 1983. The entire AONB covers 560 square miles (1,450 square kilometres).

Much of the High Weald contains the headwaters of rivers which flow outside the AONB (such as the Medway, Ouse and Arun), but the eastern part of the High Weald comprises the broader valleys of the lower reaches of the Brede, Rother and Tillingham, which meet the sea at Rye Harbour.

The coast brings its own distinctive landform, seen most dramatically in the sandstone and clay cliffs at Fairlight, but such features are very localised and atypical of the mostly inland High Weald. Nevertheless, coastal habitats hold a different and interesting flora, and so should not be overlooked.

coastal cliffs

planted woodland

Ashdown Forest occupies a significant part of the AONB. Although never a continuous forest in the modern context of the word, much of the area has been woodland for centuries. Areas defined as ancient woodland do exist here, although it is likely that most of the woodland has been in existence for no more than 300 years, since the time of the enclosures. Individual trees may be much older and date from the ancient woodland cover.

Lowland heath — a mixture of heather heath, dominated by ling (*Calluna vulgaris*) and bracken, and grass heath — is the dominant habitat of Ashdown Forest. When grazing was widespread, the heather was kept short promoting the growth of young shoots, but since the reduction in grazing, older and senescent plants have become widespread. Cutting on a cycle to maintain heather is now practised, and cutting is also used to reduce the spread of bracken so as to allow finer grasses to establish.

Reservoirs such as Ardingly, Bewl Water, Weir Wood and Darwell have been created in the valleys of the Weald. Although their open expanses of water hold little interest for plant hunters, their margins form a valuable habitat, as do the region's smaller lakes. Elsewhere across the High Weald, ponds and wetlands flow into small streams, each of these habitats having a unique flora.

Semi-natural and managed woodland extend across significant parts of the High Weald. Apart from Ashdown Forest, other smaller woodlands are common, many of these on public and private estates that still make up a significant proportion of the land area. The National Trust, Woodland Trust, Royal Society for the Protection of Birds and the Royal Botanic Gardens, Kew all manage substantial estates and reserves in the Weald. Coppiced hazel and sweet chestnut woodland in the Weald forms another valuable man-made habitat, where dappled shade and open rides linked by arching shoots allow butterflies and dormice easy passage.

Wakehurst is managed by the Royal Botanic Gardens, Kew, but unlike its sister garden in London, the estate at Wakehurst includes a wide variety of natural and man-made habitats. Large parts of the gardens and woodlands are native oak woodland, interplanted with exotic trees and shrubs. Wakehurst is also home to the Loder Valley Nature Reserve, which surrounds one arm of the Ardingly Reservoir. Created in 1978, specifically to conserve the flora and fauna of the Weald, Loder Valley was one of the first nature reserves to be opened as part of a botanic garden and it remains an exemplar of habitat conservation.

wetlands

lowland heath, Ashdown Forest

Outcrops of sandstone, known locally as sandrock, appear across the High Weald. In some places, such as Rock Walk at Wakehurst, these have been modified by previous owners to create a picturesque walk. In others, the rocks remain in their natural state. The damp sandstone is a good habitat for lower non-flowering plants (cryptogams), including the nationally rare Tunbridge filmy fern (*Hymenophyllum tunbrigense*), but the soft stone is susceptible to erosion and damage.

Ghyll woodland is a characteristic feature of the High Weald. These deep valleys formed within the sandstone are constantly moist and many have streams at their base. As the orientation of each valley changes, alterations to light and shade provide differing and specific habitats for some of the Weald's most unusual plants.

ghyll woodland

MANAGING THE ENVIRONMENT

Managing the environment of the Weald is nothing new. Over thousands of years, woodland and farmland have been carefully altered and managed for particular aims. Over time, traditional practices resulted in the formation of particular habitats, such as hay meadows where wildflowers thrive. Changes to these ways of caring for land, particularly the mechanisation that has occurred since the Second World War, have fundamentally altered many ancient habitats. This has resulted in a loss of biodiversity, which is something that current land managers are trying to reverse.

Across the High Weald, landowners are attempting to reverse any decline and to maximise the value of all of the diverse habitats that the area contains for plants and wildlife. Ashdown Forest has undergone a significant programme of habitat restoration over the past two decades. Widely established bracken (*Pteridium aquilinum*) suppresses competition, and wildflowers often disappear under its relentless

onslaught. To reverse this, the conservators have worked to scrape off a layer of soil from infested areas. Bracken rhizomes are removed and the new bare soil surface is then seeded with heathers collected from areas where they still thrive. Over a period of years, the heathers re-establish and other wildflowers follow them into this restored heathland habitat.

Gorse (*Ulex europaeus*) forms a good habitat for small birds, insects and other invertebrates when

woodland biodiversity

young, as it has a dense framework of thorny branches. However, it loses value as it matures because the structure opens out and reveals the centre of the plant and it suppresses other wildflowers. Periodic cutting (or in the past burning) of gorse in lowland and maritime heathland increases biodiversity significantly.

Many of the gardens and woodlands of the High Weald are carefully managed. In gardens and estates, exotic trees, shrubs and herbaceous plants are planted amongst native trees. Past schemes of clear felling and extensive conifer planting are now a thing of the past. Planted schemes no longer replace the native trees, but are interspersed within native woodland containing numerous oaks, ash and beech, as well as understorey shrubs such as hazel, hornbeam and elm. Occasionally, native oaks are harvested for their timber, but these trees are replaced with young saplings to secure a long-term future for the woods.

Most woodland is managed for the wildflowers on its floor. Cutting is carried out from August onwards to ensure that the wildflowers have seeded. This can lead to the woodlands looking a little untidy in late summer, but is good for their biodiversity. Control of bracken is an ongoing challenge for woodland managers, as it is on Ashdown Forest. Manual cutting in summer and again in winter is often the only solution possible. In sites where this has succeeded, bluebells have returned to places where they were last seen before the 1987 storm.

clearing scrub

gorse

Coppiced hazel woodland is carefully cut on a cycle to maximise the range of habitats available to wildflowers and native animals. A wide variety of plants thrive in coppiced woodland, varying from those that prefer the sunny conditions that result from cutting to those that prefer the deeper shade of fully grown hazel.

New meadows have been created in various parts of the High Weald. This is particularly true at Wakehurst, where locally sourced seed is used to maintain Wealden integrity in a succession of created meadows in Bloomers Valley, around the Millennium Seedbank, and forming Coronation Meadows.

Meadow restoration and management relies on cutting vegetation at the correct time of year. It is important that annual species have seeded before they are cut, but perennials are often cut before they set seed so that they do not come to dominate a meadow. After an initial cut for hay, grazing was the traditional method for maintaining meadows. The

restoring ponds

sheep grazing

use of sheep and cattle can also help to reduce the establishment of tree and shrub seedlings so that grassland is retained. Flocks of sheep are now used at Wakehurst and on Ashdown Forest to help in the management regime. Cattle can churn up areas, exposing patches of fresh soil in which the seedlings of rarer species can germinate.

Pond and lake restoration is also being undertaken. This ensures that open water areas are maintained for their wildlife value and prevents successional communities gradually turning ponds to damp woodland. Silt traps that are installed in slow-flowing streams and lakes ensure that each restoration has a long-term future.

NATIVE OR NATURALISED?

This is a tricky question to answer. Just what is a British native plant? Although most of our flora is unquestionably native, having been in the countryside since the last ice age, there are plants that have arrived through the interventions of people. Some of these date from the Roman occupation or possibly even from the Iron Age, whereas others are Victorian and twentieth-century escapes from cultivation.

Many attractive garden plants have adapted remarkably well to Sussex and have made their way out of gardens. In some cases, these alien invaders do no harm. Purple toothwort (*Lathraea clandestina*) is a native of southern Europe and lives off the roots of trees but does not damage them. However, some plants (such as Japanese knotweed,

Fallopia japonica) are highly invasive and hard to control, whereas others (including giant hogweed, *Heracleum mantegazzianum*) are potentially harmful. *Rhododendron ponticum*, a plant introduced by Victorian gardeners from the Caucasus, has proven to be highly competitive. It suppresses the growth of virtually any other plant nearby, so across the Weald, this species of rhododendron has been systematically removed to allow native plants to thrive.

Most naturalised plants are here because of accidents of history. Persian speedwell (*Veronica persica*) was introduced in the 1800s and produces vivid blue flowers in spring and early summer, whereas American speedwell (*Veronica peregrina*), which has flowers so small that they can hardly be seen, arrived in the late twentieth century.

purple toothwort

hybrid bluebell

Rhododendron ponticum

yellow rattle

American speedwell

Persian speedwell

Although yellow rattle (*Rhinanthus minor*) is found in many Wealden meadows, it is not native to all. At Wakehurst, artificially introduced yellow rattle in the meadows of the Millennium Seed Bank has now spread into many parts of the estate. Where horticulturists and conservators know of potential risks, they strive to prevent further spread.

The hybrid between our native bluebell and Spanish bluebell (*Hyacinthoides × massartiana*) can spread rapidly, so any hybrid plants are immediately removed from large public gardens. Ponds can become dominated by Canadian waterweed (*Elodea canadensis*) or by New Zealand pygmyweed (*Crassula helmsii*), and quantities of these plants often need to be reduced to allow natives to survive.

HABITATS

GARDENS

The gardens of the High Weald may appear manicured and without a plant out of place, but all is not as it seems. The horticultural teams carefully manage these areas to encourage native plants alongside exotic collections. Areas of naturalised bulbs are allowed to grow uncut until summer, encouraging meadow wildflowers to grow. Even carefully cut grass has its complement of low-growing wildflowers, and in selected areas of each garden, a less regimented approach allows wildflowers and ornamentals to mix harmoniously. In fact some wildflowers, like bluebells and foxgloves, refuse to give up even where gardeners do try to remove them.

GARDENS

The gardens of the High Weald are undeniably beautiful at any time of year, with ornamental garden varieties and botanical specimens collected throughout the twentieth century carefully planted for their aesthetic value. However, amongst these plants are native wildflowers suited to these conditions. Gardens provide some valuable habitats for wildflowers that are often obtained at a premium elsewhere.

Closely mown grass often appears to be a monoculture, where only certain types of grass can survive. Whilst this may be true for fine lawns, most mown grass is not so closely managed and low-growing species thrive here, where there is less competition. Examples include common daisy (*Bellis perennis*), dandelion (*Taraxacum officinale*), lesser trefoil (*Trifolium dubium*), creeping St John's wort (*Hypericum humifusum*), mouse-ear hawkweed (*Pilosella officinarum*) and thyme-leaved speedwell (*Veronica serpyllifolia*). In some grass areas, false oxlip (*Primula × polyantha*) can be seen. Where primrose (*Primula vulgaris*) and cowslip (*Primula veris*) are planted for their spring colour, they can hybridise and false oxlip appears.

lesser trefoil

daisy

dandelion

hairy bitter cress

mouse-ear hawkweed

Beds and borders will always provide a home to weed species, no matter how hard horticulturists try to eradicate them. So plants like procumbent pearlwort (*Sagina procumbens*), hairy bitter cress (*Cardamine hirsuta*) and wavy bitter cress (*Cardamine flexuosa*) all appear regularly despite the gardeners' best efforts. These plants were uncommon in Britain until the rise of garden centres and container-grown plants. The open compost used for our garden plants is exactly the right medium for the germination of bitter cress seed. Add this to bitter cress's explosive seed distribution mechanism and you have a perfect combination to allow these three species to travel across the country, thanks to human intervention.

creeping St John's wort

Other weeds of borders include groundsel (*Senecio vulgaris*) and cleavers or goosegrass (*Galium aparine*), the latter with its hooked leaves able to cling to shrubs and tiny white flowers in spring. The fruits are also hooked and use animal fur (and clothes) to distribute the plant. The introduced pink purslane (*Claytonia sibirica*), with attractive pink star-like flowers and fleshy leaves, has spread through many of the local gardens. Several alien species of sorrel can also be found as weeds of established beds and borders: procumbent yellow-sorrel (*Oxalis corniculata*) has small yellow flowers and usually purple leaves (although green-leaved forms are known); upright yellow-sorrel (*Oxalis stricta*) is also yellow flowered but always green leaved, larger and with a laxer habit; whereas large-flowered pink-sorrel (*Oxalis debilis*) has bright pink flowers.

Purple flowers with no leaves appear in spring at the bases of maples and some other trees. These are the blooms of purple toothwort (*Lathraea clandestina*), an introduced plant from Europe that obtains its nutrients from the roots of certain tree species, but appears to do no lasting harm to them.

Walls and other garden features also help several wildflowers to thrive. In crevices in the old stone and brick walls, ivy-leaved toadflax (*Cymbalaria muralis*) can grow alongside small ferns. Ivy-leaved speedwell (*Veronica hederifolia* subsp. *hederifolia* and subsp. *lucorum*) grows in the same way, clinging on in tiny gaps amongst the capping stones on walls. On the Horsham slate roofs of older buildings, polypody ferns are joined by white stonecrop (*Sedum album*) and the minute annual rue-leaved saxifrage (*Saxifraga tridactylites*).

ivy-leaved toadflax

coltsfoot

pink purslane

Damp soil near water features, where staff and volunteers labour to remove weeds, also forms a prime habitat for a range of species. Coltsfoot (*Tussilago farfara*) spreads by underground rhizomes, so needs open areas to thrive. Its yellow flowers appear in spring before the leaves. In streams, a range of uncommon lower plants (cryptogams) such as liverworts and mosses are often joined by monkeyflower (*Mimulus guttatus*) and brooklime (*Veronica beccabunga*). Some of these plants, such as monkeyflower and watercress (*Nasturtium officinale*), were almost certainly planted in gardens at some time in the past and have since naturalised. Along the sides of streams in the gardens, colonies of native opposite-leaved golden saxifrage (*Chrysosplenium oppositifolium*) and introduced New Zealand willowherb (*Epilobium brunnescens*) thrive.

New Zealand willowherb

Any open area is a good host for willowherbs. These plants have feathery seeds that are blown for long distances by the wind and it's not for nothing that their American common name is fireweed, as the seeds blow into, and germinate in, areas ravaged by fires. On the Wealden estates, open areas are more likely to be created by horticulturists who brush cut brambles or weed beds. Several similar willowherb species will quickly make their homes here, including rosebay willowherb (*Chamerion angustifolium*), American willowherb (*Epilobium ciliatum*), great willowherb (*Epilobium hirsutum*), broad-leaved willowherb (*Epilobium montanum*), short-fruited willowherb (*Epilobium obscurum*), hairy willowherb (*Epilobium parviflorum*) and square-stalked willowherb (*Epilobium tetragonum*).

Beds cleared for annuals or for planting next season can act as hosts for a range of wildflowers. A number of speedwell species will thrive here, spreading quickly as they can flower and seed within a few weeks of germination. Wall speedwell (*Veronica arvensis*), round-leaved speedwell (*Veronica filiformis*), grey field-speedwell (*Veronica polita*) and common speedwell (*Veronica officinalis*) all grow in this habitat, along with common forget-me-not (*Myosotis arvensis*). Scarlet pimpernel (*Anagallis arvensis*) is an annual, so will also appear where cultivated beds reduce competition. Beds that are left for longer can see the arrival of moth mullein (*Verbascum blattaria*) and common mullein (*Verbascum thapsus*). These plants are biennials, flowering and seeding in their second year, when their towering spikes of yellow flowers attract pollinators.

black bryony

corn sowthistle

common mullein

woody nightshade

In long-established areas where plants are left undisturbed, longer-lived wildflowers will appear. Black bryony (*Dioscorea communis*) is a perennial with large underground tubers. Its twining stems and bright red fruits are a common sight in gardens as this plant is very difficult to remove once the tubers are established. Woody nightshade (*Solanum dulcamara*) scrambles through shrubs and bears purple nodding flowers followed by bright red berries. At the margins of cultivated areas, there are often large groups of cherry laurel (*Prunus laurocerasus*) and cherry plum (*Prunus cerasifera*). Some of these were planted as windbreaks in the past, but in many cases, the small black fruits have been spread by birds and new plants have established without planting. Similarly, although really a weed, corn sowthistle (*Sonchus arvensis*) is a beautiful plant with large bright-yellow flower heads, which can easy become established where allowed to do so. It spreads by underground rhizomes and can be really hard to eradicate from beds and borders.

The quality of horticulture in the garden areas of the Weald estates is always high, and staff and volunteers continually strive to improve their standards. Despite the apparently manicured gardens, wildflowers still thrive here through careful management. This just shows how our native plants can find a habitat to grow in even in the most unlikely of places.

PLANTED WOODLAND

Many Wealden estates have extensive planted woodlands. Rare exotic trees, often collected by famous plant hunters, have been added to native woodland to create an ornamental resource that now holds valuable specimen trees. However, all of these exotic specimens can be seen growing amongst native woodland rather than replacing it. All of the natural wildflowers are retained and the woods are usually cut late in the summer or autumn to allow wildflower seeds to be shed. This enhances biodiversity in many ways and maximises the value of the arboreta for wild and exotic plants alike.

PLANTED WOODLAND

Planted woodlands cover a surprisingly large fraction of the land of the High Weald. Large private estates have been systematically planted with both native and exotic trees over a century or more of overseas collecting. Some, such as the arboreta at Wakehurst, are amongst the finest woodlands in the south-east of England. Exotic trees from temperate climates are planted in a geographic system, so that trees and shrubs from the same parts of the globe are grouped together. This gives a flavour of the woodland around the world, but the floor of these areas remains a haven for British native wildflowers.

Many wildflowers prefer the shaded environment of woodland, whether that be native ancient woodland or closely managed areas such as coppice or planted arboreta. The main differences between these woodland types is not in the fundamental habitat but in the way that they are managed. Most planted woodlands are cut at least annually, usually through the autumn or winter. This clears the growth of summer away, allowing more light to reach the ground and reducing available nutrients that would otherwise accumulate as leaves decay.

Areas dominated by the introduced *Rhododendron ponticum* are gradually being cleared in most of the High Weald planted woodlands, a policy actively encouraged by Natural England. This plant suppresses the growth of all competition and the dense shade under its evergreen canopy provides too little light for the growth of any wildflowers. Bracken (*Pteridium aquilinum*) acts in a similar

woodland floor

bush vetch

musk mallow

way, even producing toxic compounds from its underground shoots to reduce competition from other plants. Bracken can be gradually pushed back to the margins of the woodlands by cutting in both summer and winter. Where this management regime is successful, vast drifts of English bluebell (*Hyacinthoides non-scripta*) are a magnificent sight in spring. Where the ground is sloping and free-draining, a wide range of spring-flowering species can be seen, including the white flowers of garlic mustard (*Alliaria petiolata*) and cow parsley (*Anthriscus sylvestris*). White deadnettle (*Lamium album*) is less common, but can be found in the spring woodlands. Very occasionally, an apple tree (*Malus pumila*), probably established many years ago from a discarded core, may be seen in flower.

Some woodland clearings are almost meadow-like, with sanicle (*Sanicula europaea*), bush vetch (*Vicia sepium*), red campion (*Silene dioica*) and wood forget-me-not (*Myosotis sylvatica*) growing amongst the grasses and sedges. Lady's smock or cuckoo flower (*Cardamine pratensis*) can be seen growing in large numbers, especially in more open woods. This welcome sight is followed later in the year by scenes featuring other species, as these areas become a patchwork of orpine (*Sedum telephium*), wood avens (*Geum urbanum*), spear thistle (*Cirsium vulgare*), musk mallow (*Malva moschata*) and tutsan (*Hypericum androsaemum*).

red campion

On steep rocky outcrops, there is less competition and smaller plants can establish successfully. These include the beautiful wood sorrel (*Oxalis acetosella*) with leaves of three heart-shaped leaflets and bell-like white flowers. Wild strawberry (*Fragaria vesca*) and lesser celandine (*Ficaria verna*) can be found here, their flowers appearing before the tree leaves develop and light levels fall.

Honeysuckle (*Lonicera periclymenum*) can often be seen scrambling through the planted shrubs, and hedge bindweed (*Calystegia sepium*) will establish very quickly if not removed. These plants do little damage in the woodlands, although along with woody nightshade (*Solanum dulcamara*), they are often checked periodically by woodland staff and volunteers and removed when becoming a problem. In denser shade, small colonies of lords and ladies or cuckoo-pint (*Arum maculatum*) can often be found in spring, with their bright red fruit attracting birds later in the year.

wild strawberry

honeysuckle

hedge bindweed

devil's bit scabious

sanicle

lords and ladies

goldenrod

goat's rue

wood forget-me-not

Along the woodland fringes of damper areas, teasel (*Dipsacus fullonum*) and goat's rue (*Galega officinalis*) can become established. It is unlikely that either is native to the High Weald, but on these sunny slopes, they are thriving and attract honey bees and other pollinators. Late summer sees the welcome appearance of devil's bit scabious (*Succisa pratensis*), goldenrod (*Solidago virgaurea*), bristly ox-tongue (*Helminthotheca echioides*) and two species of hawkweed (*Hieracium sabaudum* and *Hieracium lachenalii* subsp. *argillaceum*) through the woodlands. Ling or heather (*Calluna vulgaris*) is another well-known late summer wildflower, with large colonies being established where the plants are left uncut in winter. Ling is often joined by bilberry (*Vaccinium myrtillus*) on the sandier acidic soils. The sandstone outcrops where these species thrive are also suited to broom (*Cytisus scoparius*).

NATURAL WOODLAND

The native woodlands of the Weald are amongst the most
beautiful parts of Kent and Sussex and always worth seeing.
Careful management of these seemingly natural areas
maximises the benefits that they provide to their plants
and animals and ensures that a wide range of wildflowers
is conserved. Dedicated woodland reserves under various
owners are an essential part of the Weald, with Wakehurst
amongst the first botanic gardens to incorporate a nature
reserve specifically dedicated to our native flora. The mosaic
of plants found there includes some of the rarest Wealden
wildflowers and constantly changes with the seasons.

NATURAL WOODLAND

Natural woodland on the High Weald is often formed of small areas in a patchwork with other habitats. It may be found between planted and managed woodlands or between more open areas of heathland or meadow. Generally, natural woodland is not actively managed, although historically these woodlands formed a source of charcoal for iron smelting, which led to effective management to maximise timber production. Today, management and intervention levels are much lower in natural woodlands than in planted arboreta and coppice, although cattle are being used to keep the woodland floor open in many places, including Ashdown Forest.

Natural woodland will tend to be dominated by a single species, but contains many more. In much of the High Weald, oak (*Quercus robur*) is the dominant tree, towering over smaller species and shrubs. On the acidic soils of Ashdown Forest, Scots pine (*Pinus sylvestris*) can form woodland stands with silver birch (*Betula pendula*) and shrubs beneath. Where the woodland is very wet, ash (*Fraxinus excelsior*) often becomes the dominant tree as this species will tolerate much wetter conditions, where it can be joined by alder (*Alnus glutinosa*). The arrival of ash dieback, an airborne disease of ash trees, may make the future for ash woodlands very uncertain. Silver birch is a pioneer species, moving into new habitats

cattle grazing in Ashdown forest

rowan

blackthorn

hawthorn

and beginning the process of woodland formation. It has a relatively short life for a tree, rarely exceeding 100 years, so is usually absent from very old woodland except in clearings and at the margins.

Many of the species encountered in more managed planted woodlands will be found here as well. However, there are plants of native woodland that can be found in few other habitats, and these are described here.

Flowering native trees including rowan (*Sorbus aucuparia*) and whitebeam (*Sorbus aria*) bear heads of small white flowers in spring and brilliant red berries in autumn. Crab apple (*Malus sylvestris*) is quite common in the woodlands where both

hawthorn (*Crataegus monogyna*) and its natural hybrid (*Crataegus × media*) grow into small trees. Holly (*Ilex aquifolium*) can develop into a magnificent evergreen tree, but is more commonly encountered as a shrub. Its small white flowers in spring are followed, on female plants, by scarlet berries.

Wild cherry (*Prunus avium*) and blackthorn (*Prunus spinosa*) are amongst the first woodlanders to flower in spring. Elderberry (*Sambucus nigra*) and guelder rose (*Viburnum opulus*) bloom a little later, both with flat heads of white flowers attracting many pollinating insects. Birds devour their berries in autumn, with the black shiny fruits of elderberry contrasting the bright glassy red fruits of guelder rose.

Field rose (*Rosa arvensis*) and dog rose (*Rosa canina*) will both be encountered scrambling amongst other shrubs to reach the light. The beautiful white or pink flowers of these species appear in early summer, and they can be distinguished by the length of their styles. Dog roses have short styles, so that the stigmas rest on the ovary at the centre of the flower. In field rose, long styles carry the stigmas clear of the surrounding stamens.

Although much less common, dogwood (*Cornus sanguinea*), red currant (*Ribes rubrum*) and gooseberry (*Ribes uva-crispa*) can all be found in these woodlands. On acidic sandy soils, gorse (*Ulex europaeus*) establishes and its bright yellow flowers appear almost throughout the year, hence the old expression "when gorse is out of bloom kissing is out of fashion".

On the woodland floor, umbels of starry white flowers appear amongst the broad green leaves of ramsons (*Allium ursinum*), with their unmistakable aroma of onions. Other spring blooms include the

dog rose

ramson

bright blue flowers of germander speedwell (*Veronica chamaedrys*) and the white flowers of greater stitchwort (*Stellaria holostea*). Where there is less competition from taller species, early dog violet (*Viola reichenbachiana*) is amongst the earliest to flower. Sometimes the delicate pale mauve flowers of early dog violet never open at all, developing straight into green three-sided pods. The flowering of this violet is closely followed by that of dog violet (*Viola riviniana*), which grows in natural woodland as well as in more open habitats, such as coppice and planted arboreta.

In a few favoured places, you will find wild daffodil (*Narcissus pseudonarcissus*), its trumpet-shaped flowers showing the ancestry of our garden varieties. The flowering of wood speedwell (*Veronica montana*), valerian (*Valeriana officinalis*) and columbine (*Aquilegia vulgaris*) follows that of the daffodils in some woodlands, with cut-leaved cranesbill (*Geranium dissectum*) and herb Robert (*Geranium robertianum*) flowering over a long period into summer.

wild daffodil

early dog violet

greater stitchwort

cut-leaved cranesbill

bitter vetch

Amongst the many wildflowers in the woodlands, heath groundsel (*Senecio sylvaticus*) and sticky groundsel (*Senecio viscosus*) are very similar. Their small yellow flower heads are like those of common groundsel but have a few ray florets surrounding each head. Yellow pimpernel (*Lysimachia nemorum*) is a prostrate perennial, which develops bright yellow star-like flowers from spring into summer. Bitter vetch (*Lathyrus linifolius*) and hedge bedstraw (*Galium mollugo*) are less frequent, but common mallow (*Malva sylvestris*) can be found widely, its large pink or mauve flowers each marked with darker lines and guides for pollinators.

If you are lucky, you may find wild thyme (*Thymus praecox* subsp. *polytrichus*) or ivy-leaved bellflower (*Wahlenbergia hederacea*) on slopes and rocky places. These delicate ground-hugging plants will rarely grow to more than a few centimetres high. Wild thyme bears heads of deep mauve flowers whereas ivy-leaved bellflower has individual blue trumpet-like blossoms.

hoary ragwort

common ivy

violet helleborine

Amongst the flowers of summer in Wealden woodlands, two species of orchid can be chanced upon in deep shade. Broad-leaved helleborine (*Epipactis helleborine*) and violet helleborine (*Epipactis purpurata*) are both very uncommon, with blooms carried on elegant tall heads. They can be hard to tell apart in isolation, but violet helleborine has narrower leaves with a purplish underside and its flowers have a whitish lip, whereas broad-leaved helleborine has flowers with a purple lip.

As autumn approaches, further woodlanders bloom. The brown flowers of figwort (*Scrophularia nodosa*) attract wasps as pollinators, while heads of white or pink hedge parsley (*Torilis japonica*) suit a range of insects. Deep purple flowers on wood woundwort (*Stachys sylvatica*) accompany a distinct foxy aroma. Hoary ragwort (*Senecio erucifolius*), although similar to common ragwort, has narrower, more divided leaves. Wood sage (*Teucrium scorodonia*) and enchanter's nightshade (*Circaea lutetiana*) are common in shady corners, and in a few places, hop

(*Humulus lupulus*) can be found climbing through shrubs. Lesser skullcap (*Scutellaria minor*), with its delicate hooded mauve flowers, is found in a few woodlands. Last to flower in autumn is common ivy (*Hedera helix*), whose green flowers in umbels attract wasps, bees and late-flying butterflies, and with berries that follow sustaining birds through winter.

COPPICE WOODLAND

Coppice woodland is an artificial man-made habitat of great value to wildlife. Certain trees and shrubs will allow their stems to be cut almost to ground level and then will re-grow shoots from the base. This habit allows coppice woodland to develop, generating material for pea sticks to support flowers and vegetables, hurdles, besom brooms and, through burning of the larger branches, charcoal. Cyclical cutting develops a patchwork across the woodland, with sunny newly cut coppice gradually becoming more shaded. A wide range of plants and animals make this their preferred home and thrive under these conditions.

COPPICE WOODLAND

The coppice woodland across the Weald is carefully managed for both production and wildlife. Hazel, willow, poplar, alder and sweet chestnut can all be coppiced, with the intervals between cutting depending on the species concerned and the size of wood required. Hazel is cut almost to the ground every nine years and is the High Weald's most common coppice species. Sweet chestnut has a longer cutting interval, and the long straight shoots that result can be used for palings and rails for fencing. Poplar coppice is uncommon, as the wood produced is of limited value, and similarly, alder coppice will only establish on very wet sites, making harvesting more demanding.

Many traditional products are the result of centuries of coppice management, with the Sussex trug perhaps the most iconic of this region. Charcoal is probably the most economically significant product from coppice woodland. The iron smelting industry in the Weald was founded on an ability to make high-temperature fires that could be used to smelt the iron out of its ore stone. These temperatures can be achieved using charcoal fires, for which a copious supply of charcoal and the coppice woodland that produces it are needed. Products as varied as walking sticks and eel and fish traps can all be fashioned from coppiced wood, explaining the longevity of these highly attractive woodlands throughout the High Weald.

old coppice woodland

For wildlife, the advantage of coppicing is the gradual transition from freshly cut woodland, where sunlight streams in and the ground warms up, to mature sections where there is dense shade. Plants thrive in different conditions, so wildflowers that have remained dormant suddenly spring into life after cutting. The warm sunlight and abundant wildflowers found in these newly coppiced sections draw butterflies, which use the sunny rides that dissect shaded areas to travel between flowers. Dormice use the closed hazel canopy to travel across the woodland. They are almost entirely dependent on hazel for their food, so only really thrive in these woodland habitats.

Although many of the plants found in coppice can also be seen in both natural and planted woodland, this specific habitat does favour the plants described here, and coppice is the habitat in which they are most likely to be seen. In spring, coppice woodland is a joy to experience, with wood anemone (*Anemone nemorosa*) and primrose (*Primula vulgaris*) contrasting with the purple flowers of ground ivy (*Glechoma hederacea*) and common dog violet (*Viola riviniana*).

wood spurge

primrose

common dog violet

creeping Jenny

A little later, yellow archangel (*Lamium galeobdolon*) and wood spurge (*Euphorbia amygdaloides*) form drifts of yellow or green flowers, before these flowers are in turn replaced by those of creeping Jenny (*Lysimachia nummularia*). In favoured places, the glorious flower spikes of early purple orchid (*Orchis mascula*) will be seen in April or early May.

As summer advances, flamboyant spikes of foxglove (*Digitalis purpurea*) tower over young hazel, while our three native berries, bramble (*Rubus fruticosus*), raspberry (*Rubus idaeus*) and dewberry (*Rubus*

early purple orchid

bramble

foxglove

lesser burdock

caesius) flower repeatedly until autumn, attracting bees and butterflies to their bright white or pink blooms. As summer fades, common hemp nettle (*Galeopsis tetrahit*) comes into flower, producing mauve blooms amongst its toothed leaves.

Lesser burdock (*Arctium minus*), with huge leaves and dull purple flowers, often grows in these woods. These flowers are popular with bumble bees and the seed heads with goldfinches, but beware the bracts on these heads – they have evolved to hook onto animal fur but will also catch your clothing.

Coppice woodland is usually planted beneath oak standard trees. These are harvested on a much longer cycle than the hazel or sweet chestnut below, forming a valuable resource not only for the woodland owner but also for wildlife. The patchwork nature of coppice and the wildflowers that thrive here are also a magnet for animals. Uncommon butterflies, such as White Admiral and Purple Emperor, can be seen drifting between the oak trees and occasionally dropping to feed on bramble flowers in summer. Numerous woodland birds can be seen on the oaks and amongst the seeds and berries of wildflowers, and badgers and foxes are frequent members of the coppice ecosystem.

GHYLL WOODLAND

Ghyll woodland is a particular habitat, unique to steep-sided valleys. Although ghyll woodlands are more common in the west and uplands of Great Britain, the Weald is fortunate to have extensive areas of this habitat type. These beautiful valleys are densely wooded and usually have a trickling stream at their bottom. The steep-sided valleys lend themselves to uncommon wildflowers and, more particularly, to rare lower plants. They have never been used by humans as the terrain is too difficult to work, so these are often amongst the most ancient and valuable woodlands of the Weald.

GHYLL WOODLAND

Ghyll woodland is the term used to describe woodland on steep-sided valleys. The majority of such woodlands are found in upland areas of Great Britain and towards the west coast. Finding this habitat in south-east England is therefore an unexpected surprise, given the generally drier climate of this region. Over 6% of the High Weald in Sussex is classed as ghyll woodland, a rare habitat type and unique landscape feature of this part of Sussex. Ghyll woodland in these terms specifically applies to the woodland found in the Sandstone and Hastings Beds of the High Weald.

Owing to their isolation and enclosed nature, ghylls have a unique microclimate, and are often rich in lower plants such as bryophytes and other moisture-loving species. Ghyll woodlands are found in the extreme upper reaches of rivers, where springs and streams develop in small, steep, wooded valleys. The steep-sided nature of these woodlands has also ensured that many ghyll woodlands have remained relatively untouched and undisturbed by human activity.

Tree cover is provided by a mix of species similar to those found in other Wealden woodlands, but with a high proportion of silver birch (*Betula pendula*), downy birch (*Betula pubescens*) and ash (*Fraxinus excelsior*). Hawthorn (*Crataegus monogyna*), hazel (*Corylus avellana*), field maple (*Acer campestre*) and holly (*Ilex aquifolium*) are the most common

ghyll woodland

hawthorn

understorey trees or shrubs. Where the ground becomes slightly more manageable, the ghyll valleys often abut coppice woods. The presence of hazel, and sometimes sweet chestnut (*Castanea sativa*), here is therefore unsurprising, and these trees are accompanied by coppice woodland wildflowers such as primrose (*Primula vulgaris*) and yellow archangel (*Lamium galeobdolon*).

The flora found in these sites is very characteristic of that found in former Atlantic conditions. It includes lush growths of ferns (such as hay-scented buckler fern, *Dryopteris aemula*), mosses and liverworts. Many ghyll woodlands are likely to be primary woodland sites, potentially dating from the ice age. Ghyll woodlands also provide an important function within the wider river catchment because they help to capture and slow down rainfall and overland run-off. This water would otherwise have the potential to cause erosion in these steep areas. The dense shade provided by ghyll woodlands keeps streams cool, so that downstream, the water is better suited to the reproduction of a number of fish species.

sweet chestnut

field maple

yellow archangel

skunk cabbage

Himalayan balsam

The damp habitat of ghyll woodlands is vulnerable to invasive species. Both skunk cabbage (*Lysichiton americanus*), with its bright yellow spring flowers and large foliage, and Himalayan balsam (*Impatiens glandulifera*) favour stream sides. They will tolerate shady conditions and spread rapidly, threatening this unique habitat.

Wildflowers in ghyll woodland can often seem a little sparse, as the almost permanently shaded conditions allow only a restricted range of species to grow. However, one side of each valley is often cooler than the other, and so encourages a slightly different set of plants to thrive. Dog's mercury (*Mercurialis perennis*) is often widespread, producing small green flowers in early spring. These flowers are followed by those of ground ivy (*Glechoma hederacea*), wood anemone (*Anemone nemorosa*), heath dog violet (*Viola canina*) and ramsons (*Allium ursinum*), all of which flower before the leaves on the tree canopy develop fully and reduce the amount of light that reaches the woodland floor.

The permanently damp environment of the ghyll valleys encourages rarities such as ivy-leaved bellflower (*Wahlenbergia hederacea*) and Cornish

herb Robert

enchanter's nightshade

moneywort (*Sibthorpia europaea*). These will not be found in all ghyll woodlands, but you may chance upon them if lucky. More widespread, in fact present in most ghyll woodlands, are large bitter cress (*Cardamine amara*) and opposite-leaved golden saxifrage (*Chrysosplenium oppositifolium*). The former is a relative of the weedy hairy bitter cress, but with larger more attractive flowers, whereas the latter is a ground-hugging plant adorned by yellow-green flowers in flat heads in spring.

Later in summer, shade-tolerant species such as herb Robert (*Geranium robertianum*), with its pink flowers, continue to attract pollinating insects. Enchanter's nightshade (*Circaea lutetiana*) flowers in late summer or early autumn, with heads of small white flowers still visible in the deep shade. Throughout summer, the yellow flowers of wood avens (*Geum urbanum*) can be seen, and these are followed by hooked fruits that have evolved to catch in the fur of passing animals.

dog's mercury

golden saxifrage

SANDROCK

The High Weald of Sussex and Kent is unusual in the south-
east of England in having high rainfall and being very damp.
Part of the reason for the dampness is that the underlying
rocks are sandstones, which hold water. The damp rock
releases water very slowly, allowing lower plants to colonise
the surface and to remain moist even through droughts. The
sandrock habitat is highly specialised and valuable, being
home to some of Europe's most endangered plants, including
the Tunbridge filmy fern (*Hymenophyllum tunbrigense*).

SANDROCK

Sandrock habitats are highly vulnerable to damage. The Wealden sandstone rock is only hard and weatherproof when left undisturbed for several years. The exterior gradually hardens but the interior is very soft, so damage to the surface can lead to rapid erosion. Where rocks have suffered this fate, particularly in public parks and gardens, they support no plant growth. Beautiful colonies of lower plants (cryptogams) will develop if protected, so the key to retaining this wonderful habitat is to minimise disturbance and to remove invasive plants such as rhododendrons. With careful management, some of Europe's rarest plants can be encouraged.

filmy fern

eroded sandstone

sandrock

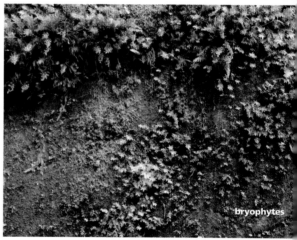

bryophytes

hard fern

A wealth of lower plants, particularly mosses and liverworts, thrive on the sandrock surface. Because the rock is porous, water constantly moves through it to evaporate at the surface. As lower plants do not have a developed root system, their water-absorbing rhizoids draw water from this damp surface for survival. Ferns are more evolved and do have true roots. They are often present on sandrock, growing in natural fissures where their roots can grow to a greater depth to absorb water and nutrients.

The nationally threatened Tunbridge filmy fern (*Hymenophyllum tunbrigense*) is a specialised fern. Its leaves are only a single cell thick, so cannot tolerate drying out, even for a short period. Clinging tightly to the always damp sandrock therefore allows this delicate fern to survive in the otherwise hostile dry climate of south-east England.

Very few wildflowers grow on sandrock. Because they have a much larger root system and often need more nutrients than lower plants, wildflowers rarely occupy this specialised habitat. In many ways this is a good thing because flowering plants are much more vigorous than mosses, liverworts and ferns. The presence of wildflowers on sandrock almost certainly means that none of the delicate lower plants can compete. Of the wildflowers that do grow on sandrock, you are most likely to find wood

wood sorrel

sorrel (*Oxalis acetosella*), which has small tubers that can overwinter in rock crevices and small leaves that do not smother smaller plants. At the bases of rock outcrops, you will often find larger ferns, such as broad buckler fern (*Dryopteris dilatata*) and hard fern (*Blechnum spicant*), along with yellow archangel (*Lamium galeobdolon*) and ground ivy (*Glechoma hederacea*).

lichens

yellow archangel

ground ivy

MEADOWS

Meadows are one of the most threatened habitats in Britain.
Over 90% of old meadow has been lost since 1945. Maintaining
existing meadows and creating new ones is a major driver in
current conservation work in the High Weald, with Wakehurst
and the Millennium Seed Bank using their expertise to help
other conservationists across the area. Cutting meadows only
after the wonderful wildflowers have seeded in mid-summer
ensures the emergence of new generations of plants in
successive years. Timing is crucial, with different wildflowers
being helped by summer or autumn cutting.

MEADOWS

The meadows of the High Weald vary in age very considerably. Some can be considered as ancient meadows, but most are much more recent. Many meadows were destroyed in the quest for food production during the Second World War and in the conversion to arable farming that followed. So, for example, at Wakehurst, the oldest meadow is Hanging Meadow in the Loder Valley Nature Reserve at 70 years or so. It has been regularly surveyed for the species in flower since Kew took over management of the Reserve in 1978, and this survey has shown gradual changes over a long period caused by the management regime and the changing climate.

Wakehurst has been working with other meadow owners in the High Weald for 20 years to establish new wildflower meadows. New meadows have been seeded and planted around the Millennium Seed Bank and in Bloomers Valley, where a variety of Wealden species were raised as plants and added to natural regeneration after regular mowing was stopped in 2005. A Coronation Meadow has since been established here, using Bedelands Reserve near Burgess Hill as a seed donor source.

Cutting meadows in July to September encourages the annuals to seed. Grazing with sheep over winter then opens up the sward to ensure that these seeds reach the soil and germinate in the next spring. In some meadows, cattle have also been used successfully to create bare areas in which annuals can establish after grazing stops in early spring.

For most meadows, the flowering year starts with the blooming of bugle (*Ajuga reptans*), dog's mercury (*Mercurialis perennis*) and ground ivy (*Glechoma hederacea*). The sunnier open situation favours cowslip (*Primula veris*) over primroses (*Primula vulgaris*), although both can be present in meadows. The flowers of barren strawberry (*Potentilla sterilis*), common mouse-ear (*Cerastium*

bugle

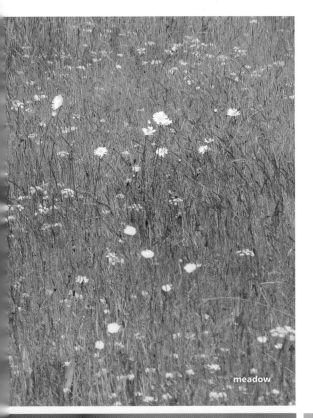

meadow

fontanum), sticky mouse-ear (*Cerastium glomeratum*) and lesser stitchwort (*Stellaria graminea*) also appear early in the year before the grasses grow taller and shade these low-growing plants.

As spring turns to early summer, three species of forget-me-not (changing forget-me-not, *Myosotis discolor*; early forget-me-not, *Myosotis ramosissima*; and tufted forget-me-not, *Myosotis laxa*) can be found in Wealden meadows. They are joined by many other native wildflowers, including red clover (*Trifolium pratense*), white clover (*Trifolium repens*), bird's foot trefoil (*Lotus corniculatus*) and, in damper areas, marsh bird's foot trefoil (*Lotus pedunculatus*). These particularly colourful flowers attract both bumble and honey bees to pollinate them.

Yellow rattle (*Rhinanthus minor*) is an annual plant that attaches itself to the roots of grasses and draws nutrients from them. As such, it reduces grass vigour in meadows and is sometimes added to the mix of species in new meadows to aid establishment.

bird's foot trefoil

red clover

white clover

Common sorrel (*Rumex acetosa*) and the smaller sheep's sorrel (*Rumex acetosella*) have delicate pink flowers that rapidly turn to seed, and the brown flowers of ribwort plantain (*Plantago lanceolata*) are a common sight in all meadow areas. Hoary plantain (*Plantago media*) is much less common and has green flowers with prominent mauve anthers. The small white umbels of pignut (*Conopodium majus*) add a delicate note amongst the grasses. Also with white flowers, heath bedstraw (*Galium saxatile*) is very similar to marsh bedstraw (*Galium palustre*) but favours drier habitats than those preferred by its water-loving relative.

Meadows reach their peak in June, when drifts of ox-eye daisy (*Leucanthemum vulgare*), meadow buttercup (*Ranunculus acris*) and creeping buttercup (*Ranunculus repens*) are joined by lower-growing silverweed (*Potentilla anserina*), tormentil (*Potentilla erecta*) and cinquefoil (*Potentilla reptans*). Hop trefoil (*Trifolium campestre*) is similarly short, whereas hairy tare (*Vicia hirsuta*), smooth tare (*Vicia tetrasperma*) and field bindweed (*Convolvulus arvensis*) use other plants as supports as they clamber into the light. Bulbous buttercup (*Ranunculus bulbosus*) is much less common than meadow or creeping buttercup, but is present in some Wealden meadows. In many of the meadow areas, common spotted orchid (*Dactylorhiza fuchsii*) is very widespread and is encouraged by cutting late in summer after the minute seed is shed. Much less common, southern marsh orchid (*Dactylorhiza praetermissa*) has larger deeper pink flowers. Not all orchids are colourful though, and twayblade (*Neottia ovata*) bears spikes of green blooms.

meadow buttercup

cinquefoil

common spotted orchid

twayblade orchid

self-heal

yarrow

marsh thistle

ragwort

Mid-summer sees a change of species that are in flower with yarrow (*Achillea millefolium*), common agrimony (*Agrimonia eupatoria*), common centaury (*Centaurium erythraea*), self-heal (*Prunella vulgaris*) and knapweed (*Centaurea nigra*) coming to dominate in meadows. Creeping thistle (*Cirsium arvense*) and marsh thistle (*Cirsium palustre*) will often be seen in flower, although creeping thistle is often removed or sprayed so that is does not outcompete other wildflowers. In a similar way, ragwort (*Jacobaea vulgaris*) is often removed as it is dangerous to livestock if eaten. Nevertheless, ragwort is a native wildflower and its parachute seeds travel long distances, so it can always be found in some places.

Perforate St John's wort (*Hypericum perforatum*), beautiful St John's wort (*Hypericum pulchrum*) and square-stalked St John's wort (*Hypericum tetrapterum*) will be seen in high summer, with their star-like yellow flowers above the oval leaves. Cat's-ear (*Hypochaeris radicata*) is very common throughout most meadows, with its yellow ray florets forming a head similar to that of dandelion but on taller stems. Smooth hawk's-beard (*Crepis capillaris*) and lesser hawkbit (*Leontodon saxatilis*) are very similar but with more divided leaves.

Dyer's greenweed (*Genista tinctoria*) and saw-wort (*Serratula tinctoria*) are less common inhabitants of meadows. Both are perennials that tolerate a regular cutting and grazing regime. Grass-leaved vetchling (*Lathyrus nissolia*) is also very uncommon. An annual, this plant has tendrils that allow it to attach to grasses and other stems and to climb towards the light, where single red flowers appear in mid-summer.

Several other pea flowers are widespread in meadows and all flower through high summer. Meadow pea (*Lathyrus pratensis*) clambers through other plants, using tendrils to secure its stems. Tufted vetch (*Vicia cracca*) is a vigorous climber, easily reaching the sunlight above meadow wildflowers or shrubs, and has brilliant purple-blue flowers in dense elongated heads. Common vetch (*Vicia sativa* subsp. *segetalis*) and narrow-leaved vetch (*Vicia sativa* subsp. *nigra*) are very similar. These are shorter plants than tufted vetch, both with purple flowers. The flowers of narrow-leaved vetch are more vibrant and of a redder shade.

Towards the end of summer, wild angelica (*Angelica sylvestris*) and hogweed (*Heracleum sphondylium*) appear amongst the other wildflowers. Both bear large flat umbels of flowers held above their broad basal leaves. Wild angelica is completely hairless, whereas hogweed is densely hairy all over, making them relatively easy to distinguish. Corn mint (*Mentha arvensis*) and its hybrid with water mint, whorled mint (*Mentha × verticillata*), can both be seen in meadows, their densely packed mauve flowers attracting bees and flies as pollinators.

cat's ear

common vetch

meadow pea

grass-leaved vetchling

betony

tufted vetch

Hemp agrimony (*Eupatorium cannabinum*) and fleabane (*Pulicaria dysenterica*) are often the most dramatic species in late summer. Hemp agrimony can grow up to 1.5 m in height, and is topped off with flat heads of mauve flowers above narrow-toothed leaves. By contrast, fleabane is a much smaller plant, rarely exceeding 30 cm. It has bright yellow daisy flowers and spreads by extensive rhizomes to form dense clumps in the damper meadows. Also late flowering is betony (*Stachys officinalis*), with bright red-purple flowers in compact heads. This species can often be seen in glades and open areas in the woodlands as it tolerates a wide range of growing conditions.

LOWLAND HEATH

Lowland heath is a rare and threatened habitat in Britain. Very poor soils, with few nutrients for plants, combine with gently undulating ground to create expanses of heath. Plants that are adapted to these conditions include heathers and many small perennial species, whose size and rate of growth is slow but whose beauty is often immense. Lowland heath is the major component of Ashdown Forest, where it is interspersed with woodland. Bracken and gorse can come to dominate heathland, so active conservation aims to manage and reduce the effects of both of these species.

LOWLAND HEATH

Several habitat types make up lowland heath. This can vary from pure ling or heather heath to pure stands of bracken (*Pteridium aquilinum*), with grass-dominated heath between the two. Heather heathland is the most interesting environment for wildflowers, with a wide range of other species being associated with this type of habitat. Short grassland is also interesting, particularly where rabbits keep the grasses very short and allow small perennial wildflowers to thrive. Bracken shades out almost all wildflowers apart from very early spring-flowering species. It is therefore vigorously controlled by those managing these heathland areas, much as it is in woodlands and meadow margins. Repeated cutting with a forage harvester or flail mower will weaken the bracken, to the point where grasses and other species eventually come to dominate.

ling

bell heather

cross-leaved heath

heathland

Heather heath in the High Weald is largely dominated by ling (*Calluna vulgaris*). This vigorous perennial is covered in pale mauve flowers in late summer, and will eventually form a scrubland habitat if allowed to grow unchecked. Periodic cutting keeps the plants shorter and allows other species to thrive while also increasing the value of the ling itself to insects and other wildlife.

Where the land is slightly drier, bell heather (*Erica cinerea*), with its deeper purple bell-shaped flowers in upright heads, will also be found. Conversely, where depressions lead to wet conditions, the heather mix changes to mostly cross-leaved heath (*Erica tetralix*). This species has delicate pink flowers in a dense terminal cluster at the end of tall flowering shoots.

Amongst the heathers, you will also find extensive areas of dwarf gorse (*Ulex minor*). This species resembles common gorse (*Ulex europaeus*) but is smaller and never grows into a large shrub. It also flowers at a different time of year. Common gorse is almost never out of flower, but it does actually stop flowering over the height of summer, when dwarf gorse comes into its own. The bright yellow pea-like flowers of dwarf gorse adorn the short spiny shoots throughout mid- to late summer. Heathland is also home to broom (*Cytisus scoparius*), a spineless shrub that produces dramatic yellow flowers in early summer.

Smaller species can grow amongst this spiny protection. Amongst them, common milkwort (*Polygala vulgaris*) has small deep blue to purple flowers, whereas the much less common heath milkwort (*Polygala serpyllifolia*) always has blue flowers and shorter broader leaves. Very occasionally, you will come across lousewort (*Pedicularis sylvatica*). This hemi-parasitic plant attaches to the roots of grasses and other plants to obtain more nutrients

lousewort

dwarf gorse

than can be produced by its own small leaves. It bears pink-lipped flowers in early summer. Another oddity of heathland is dodder (*Cuscuta epithymum*). This is another parasitic plant, but this time having no green leaves at all. It relies entirely on nutrients from the host plants that it twines around and infects with root-like haustoria. In late summer, the twining red shoots are adorned by spherical clusters of pink flowers.

Where grasses dominate the heathland, a wide range of summer-flowering wildflowers can be seen. Bright yellow cinquefoil (*Potentilla reptans*), tormentil (*Potentilla erecta*) and trailing tormentil (*Potentilla anglica*) are joined by common speedwell (*Veronica officinalis*), lesser stitchwort (*Stellaria graminea*) and pignut (*Conopodium majus*). Large patches of silverweed (*Potentilla anserina*) are often found at path edges, but some can be reluctant to flower, so

autumn hawkbit

their silvery leaves may not always be accompanied by bright yellow flowers in early summer. Milkwort (*Polygala serpyllifolia*) is also an inhabitant of these heaths, along with heath spotted orchid (*Dactylorhiza maculata*) and heath bedstraw (*Galium saxatile*). In late summer and autumn, bright yellow dandelion-like flowers are produced by autumn hawkbit (*Scorzoneroides autumnalis*), particularly on shallow slopes and path edges.

In low-lying areas, heathland can rapidly become waterlogged. Marshes and bogs will develop here, often dominated by distinctive sphagnum moss. They are frequently quite small in area, so they nestle within heather or grass heathland. A range of interesting wildflowers grow in these soggy conditions. In late spring, the early marsh orchid (*Dactylorhiza incarnata*) and southern marsh orchid (*Dactylorhiza praetermissa*) produce dramatic

common speedwell

spikes of pink or mauve flowers. These flowers are followed in high summer by those of bog asphodel (*Narthecium ossifragum*), which are delicate yellow and amongst grass-like foliage. In a few favoured localities, the nationally rare marsh gentian (*Gentiana pneumonanthe*) still thrives. Its deep blue trumpet flowers can be seen atop the stems of whorled narrow leaves in late summer. Where the ground is permanently saturated, nutrients are in poor supply and unobtainable. Where sphagnum moss but little else thrives, the two native species of sundew might

heath spotted orchid

be glimpsed. Both form small rosettes that hug the ground, with circular leaves in round-leaved sundew (*Drosera rotundifolia*) and elongated in oblong-leaved sundew (*Drosera intermedia*). The leaves are covered in sticky glandular hairs that trap and then engulf small insects that chance to land on them. The bodies of the insects are gradually digested and the nutrients absorbed by the plant. In summer, the sundews send up a single spike of small white flowers, well away from their deadly leaves so that pollinating insects don't become their next victim.

oblong-leaved sundew

southern marsh orchid

STREAMS, LAKESIDES AND WETLANDS

Rivers are at a premium in Sussex, but streams are fortunately more common. Throughout the High Weald there are natural springs where sandstone rock strata and clay soils meet, creating damp areas leading to small streams. Permanent and seasonal streams allow moisture-loving wildflowers to thrive in abundance, often producing dramatic and brightly coloured flowers through summer. Where depressions and ponds occur, wetland habitat develops. The constantly wet ground encourages swift growth in spring and these areas are dominated by lush beds of reed sweet-grass (*Glyceria maxima*), bur-reed (*Sparganium* spp.) and willows (*Salix* spp.), interspersed with wildflowers such as purple loosestrife (*Lythrum salicaria*).

STREAMS, LAKESIDES AND WETLANDS

Along the sides of streams, ponds and lakes, where the soil is always moist, a wide range of wonderful native wildflowers thrive. Some have brightly coloured flowers to attract pollinating insects, but others are more modest in stature and flower size, needing careful examination to appreciate their discreet beauty.

Yellow iris (*Iris pseudacorus*) is amongst the earliest to bloom, producing bright yellow flowers amongst the lance-like foliage. This very vigorous plant forms large clumps at the water's edge. Water forget-me-not (*Myosotis scorpioides*), with its dazzling blue flowers, can often be found amongst the stems of yellow iris and in other streamside locations where it stands out all the more.

Some of our most dramatic and fast-growing species can be found in ponds and streams. Bulrush (*Typha latifolia*) and lesser bulrush (*Typha angustifolia*) are iconic waterside plants, developing into huge clumps where left unchecked. Their distinctive brown cylindrical flower heads can be seen almost year round. In similar situations, flowering rush (*Butomus umbellatus*) and arrowhead (*Sagittaria sagittifolia*) can sometimes be found. Flowering rush has umbels of beautiful pink three-petalled flowers, whereas arrowhead bears clear white flowers in clusters.

Stream and lake margins are the favoured habitat of hemlock water dropwort (*Oenanthe crocata*), with its celery-like foliage and heads of white flowers. Unlike giant hogweed (*Heracleum mantegazzianum*), this highly poisonous plant is perfectly harmless until eaten, so can be left to flower unmolested. These wet streamsides are also the haunt of water mint (*Mentha aquatica*), meadowsweet (*Filipendula ulmaria*) and marsh bedstraw (*Galium palustre*). Ragged robin (*Silene flos-cuculi*) with serrated pink flowers and marsh valerian (*Valeriana dioica*) with smaller starry pink flowers can be found along the margins of streams and in wet grassland areas.

water forget-me-not

yellow iris

bulrush

meadowsweet

water dropwort

ragged robin

More subdued in colour, the brown hooded flowers of water figwort (*Scrophularia auriculata*) are followed at the edge of ponds and lakes by those of bistort (*Persicaria bistorta*) and water pepper (*Persicaria hydropiper*), with pink flowers, and in the open water by the similar, but altogether brighter pink flowers of amphibious bistort (*Persicaria amphibia*). Amongst the last species to bloom, gypsywort (*Lycopus europaeus*) has small white flowers amongst nettle-like leaves.

On the open edges of many reservoirs and larger lakes, the shore is dominated by a dense carpet of New Zealand pygmyweed (*Crassula helmsii*), water purslane (*Lythrum portula*) and shoreweed (*Littorella uniflora*). All of these species have tiny pink or brown flowers, and the latter two natives are often crowded out by the alien pygmyweed invader. In slow-flowing water, common water starwort (*Callitriche stagnalis*) can often be seen as the stems grow up to the surface as a starry whorl of bright green leaves.

Where the rate of flow of passing water slows to a minimum or stops altogether, water-loving plants will thrive and a wetland is created. In spring, marsh marigolds or kingcups (*Caltha palustris*) provide a dazzling display of yellow buttercup-like flowers. At this time of year, the yellow flowers of alien skunk cabbage (*Lysichiton americanus*) may been seen along streams and in wetland. This North American relative of arum lilies has spread along watercourses and is classed as an invasive alien.

gypsywort

marsh marigold

purple loosestrife

Late spring and early summer see the flowering of some less common natives in wetland areas. Careful searching will find starry white flowers of marsh stitchwort (*Stellaria uliginosa*) and deep purple marsh violet (*Viola palustris*). In very wet areas, the long stolons of bogbean (*Menyanthes trifoliata*) can spread through open water, leading to the growth of tufts of trefoil leaves and heads of fringed pink flowers at the tips. Equally vigorous is lesser spearwort (*Ranunculus flammula*), which can grow upright or procumbent. When procumbent, lesser spearwort forms roots freely at the lower nodes, through which it spreads. Spearwort leaves are lance-shaped and the flowers like those of glossy yellow buttercups. Late in summer, the pink or mauve spires of purple loosestrife (*Lythrum salicaria*) stand out clearly amongst grasses and reeds in wetlands and along damp stream banks.

COASTAL HABITATS

The High Weald may not usually be considered to include coastal habitats. However, between Hastings and Rye on the Sussex coast, the High Weald does indeed reach the sea. The plants that grow here are very different to those that grow in other Wealden habitats. They need to be adapted to resist salt-laden air and almost constant wind, and often must also cope with effective drought conditions in very free-draining soils. Some unusual and rare plants grow along this short stretch of coastline, making it a small but valuable part of the High Weald.

COASTAL HABITATS

Where the High Weald reaches the coast of East Sussex between Hastings and Rye, salt-tolerant species come into their own. Although you will find many wildflowers here that also grow happily inland, particularly weedy species that we will look at in detail in the next section, there is a particular ecosystem that thrives in this exposed and sometimes hostile environment.

Above the sandstone and clay cliffs near Fairlight, small areas of maritime heath still exist. This vegetation type is essentially a mix of species that is similar to those found in the heaths of Ashdown Forest, but with exposure to salt-laden winds, only the toughest survive. Bell heather (*Erica cinerea*) is a prominent feature of this heath habitat, but is almost lost when gorse is left uncut and bracken runs out of control. Now areas are being actively managed to keep the coarse vegetation at bay and to allow the heather to re-establish. Amongst the heather, plants such as slender thistle (*Carduus tenuiflorus*), wild carrot (*Daucus carota*) and black horehound (*Ballota nigra*) thrive here. Also growing with the heather are smaller species encouraged by rabbit grazing that keeps grasses and other vegetation short. Clovers, including alsike clover (*Trifolium hybridum*), knotted clover (*Trifolium striatum*) and hare's-foot clover (*Trifolium arvense*) grow with the shorter toothed medic (*Medicago polymorpha*). Where the competing plants are very reduced, on exposed rocky outcrops and cliff tops, thrift (*Armeria maritima*), sea plantain (*Plantago maritima*) and wild clary (*Salvia verbenaca*) flower in abundance in early summer. Field mouse-ear (*Cerastium arvense*), sea mouse-ear (*Cerastium diffusum*) and upright chickweed (*Moenchia erecta*) can be found nestling amongst short grass or scrambling at the base of shade-giving shrubs.

bell heather

wild carrot

alsike clover

thrift

coastal heath

sea holly

On the shingle raised beaches near Pett Level, a completely different set of plants is encountered. The shingle is extremely free draining, so although it is lashed by the wind and tide, it drains any water away from the plants' roots very quickly. Many are effectively growing in desert conditions and need an enormous root system to cope. In spring, the most obvious plant here is sea kale (*Crambe maritima*) with large heads of white flowers. Sea rocket (*Cakile maritima*) is similar but smaller, often with purple tinged flowers. Danish scurvygrass (*Cochlearia danica*) is a low-growing pant with masses of white four-petalled flowers at this time of year.

Later in summer, sea campion (*Silene uniflora*), sea pea (*Lathyrus japonicus* subsp. *maritimus*), greater celandine (*Chelidonium majus*) and viper's bugloss (*Echium vulgare*) create a splash of colour. By late summer, the shingle is still of interest, with the spectacular yellow flowers of horned poppy (*Glaucium flavum*) and large-flowered evening primrose (*Oenothera glazioviana*) joined by the light blue flowers of sea holly (*Eryngium maritimum*), which are surrounded by prickly foliage. Occasionally, the spreading stems of sea bindweed (*Calystegia soldanella*) creep across the shingle, adorned by large pink tubular flowers. Amongst these larger plants, the shingle will be home to plants with unassuming small flowers, including sea purslane (*Halimione portulacoides*), annual sea blite (*Suaeda maritima*), sea sandwort (*Honckenia peploides*) and sea heath (*Frankenia laevis*).

Immediately inland of the raised beaches, an entirely different habitat is created by the draining of low-lying land into canals and streams. Plants that need fresh water but are tolerant of the salt-laden air thrive here. These include tubular water dropwort (*Oenanthe fistulosa*) and soft hornwort (*Ceratophyllum submersum*). Marsh mallow (*Althaea officinalis*) has soft blue-green foliage and beautiful pink cup-shaped flowers in late summer. Its roots are the original source of mastic for marshmallow sweets.

In wetter areas where the land drops into old quarries or depressions, brookweed (*Samolus valerandi*) may be found. This relative of primroses has minute white flowers throughout the summer and shares its habitat with the introduced Alexanders (*Smyrnium olusatrum*). These substantial plants form a mass of yellow-green flower heads in late spring.

sea kale

horned poppy

As the coast nears Rye, saltmarsh conditions become more common. Low-lying land that is regularly inundated by salt water rapidly becomes saline and only those plants adapted to cope with this extreme habitat can survive and flourish. These include rock samphire (*Crithmum maritimum*), sea milkwort (*Lysimachia maritima*) and wild celery (*Apium graveolens*). Sea aster (*Aster tripolium*) produces heads of mauve daisy-like heads in late summer, whereas the rather less attractive sea wormwood (*Artemisia maritima*) bears small brown or green flowers slightly earlier. They both grow along the edges of saline streams and ditches.

FARMS AND WASTELAND

Although the High Weald is remarkably rich in natural and semi-natural habitats, farms still abound across the area and wasteland is a consequence both of farming and habitation. The edges of paths, bare areas used to store machines and equipment, field margins and the surrounds of buildings provide places for tough pioneer plants. Often these plants thrive in highly fertilised ground where meadow and woodland plants fail to survive. Some are certainly weeds, but then a weed is only a plant in an undesired place and there is space for all across the High Weald.

FARMS AND WASTELAND

Grouping farms and wasteland together might seem a bit strange. However, all farms have patches of wasteland at field margins, around buildings and along tracks. The margins of roads and tracks elsewhere also fall into the wasteland category. Wherever they may appear, wasteland and farms are home to some tough plants that thrive in the particular conditions provided by these habitats.

These are often species that thrive where nutrient levels are very high. Ironically, the decay of plant material generates enormous amounts of nutrient for other plants, particularly nitrogen. So, if cut debris is stacked habitually in one place, the ground here becomes nutrient-rich — ideal for plants such as stinging nettle (*Urtica dioica*) and small nettle

(*Urtica urens*). This is why these species will also appear elsewhere if cut debris, particularly grass, is dumped rather than being taken to a composting site.

Where plant debris is stacked and composted at the top of a slope, nutrient levels will rise in all the ground below. Given that the High Weald is almost all slopes, this means that many of these nitrogen-tolerant species flourish across many farms and estates, particularly near buildings. Common orache (*Atriplex patula*), redshank (*Persicaria maculosa*) and equal-leaved knotgrass (*Polygonum arenastrum*) thrive in these conditions, alongside scentless mayweed (*Tripleurospermum inodorum*) with its white daisy flowers. Docks, such as curled dock (*Rumex crispus*), broad-leaved dock (*Rumex*

stinging nettle

red deadnettle

obtusifolius) and wood dock (*Rumex sanguineus*) enjoy nutrient-rich soils. As perennials, these plants will establish when the conditions are less suited to most wildflowers, but continue to grow strongly even if nutrient levels later fall, hence they may cause problems if present in new meadows. Mugwort (*Artemisia vulgaris*) is a similar perennial that can survive in marginal places and is often found on road verges, where its salt tolerance is an advantage. A similar tough constitution allows great plantain (*Plantago major*) and yellow-flowered common yellow rocket (also known as winter cress) (*Barbarea vulgaris*) to thrive in these places.

Short-lived annuals and ephemerals are well suited to growth on these temporary sites. As pioneers, they have seed that travels long distances or can survive dormant in the soil for many years until an opportunity presents itself. That's why freshly disturbed ground, where new buildings are erected or roads constructed, rapidly fills with an array of wildflowers that may not have been seen at the site for many years. Red deadnettle (*Lamium purpureum*), thale cress (*Arabidopsis thaliana*) and shepherd's purse (*Capsella bursa-pastoris*) will often dominate open bare areas in early spring, to be replaced by chickweed (*Stellaria media*), annual pearlwort (*Sagina apetala* including subsp. *erecta*) and pineapple weed (*Matricaria discoidea*) as summer progresses. Three-nerved sandwort (*Moehringia trinervia*), hairy buttercup (*Ranunculus sardous*), lesser swine cress (*Lepidium didymum*) and petty spurge (*Euphorbia peplus*) can be found here. The gardener's old bane, groundsel (*Senecio vulgaris*), can establish flower and seed in a matter of weeks, so making it an ideal member of this short-lived community. Black medic (*Medicago lupulina*) is adorned by heads of small yellow flowers and spotted leaves. Where the soil is wet, the silvery leaves and small brown flowers of marsh cudweed (*Gnaphalium uliginosum*) will often appear in late summer.

scentless mayweed

pineapple weed

lesser swine cress

prickly lettuce

marsh cudweed

common sowthistle

At the edges of buildings, the cracks and gaps between paving and walls can be home to nipplewort (*Lapsana communis*) and wall lettuce (*Lactuca muralis*). These rather similar relatives of daisies both have small yellow flowers that rapidly produce numerous seeds on parachutes to aid dispersal. Prickly lettuce (*Lactuca serriola*) is a larger but similar plant and has the same habit, growing very fast to produce seed before conditions worsen or drought becomes intolerable in these marginal habitats.

Sow thistles are pioneers of these waste places. Prickly sowthistle (*Sonchus asper*) and common sowthistle (*Sonchus oleraceus*) both seed freely and grow as overwintering annuals. Their seeds germinate in autumn, developing into a flat rosette over winter that builds up reserves of nutrient while competition is reduced. Then, in spring, the plant grows rapidly to flower and seed.

A similar quick-growing habit can be seen in black nightshade (*Solanum nigrum*), whose white flowers and barely developed buds are present alongside ripe black fruit on older branches. This habit ensures the distribution of the seed even if conditions suddenly change for the worse before the plant has grown fully. Where waste areas remain for a longer period, perennial species can establish. Woody nightshade or bittersweet (*Solanum dulcamara*) looks very similar to black nightshade, but has purple flowers followed by red berries. This plant is much larger though, growing to a metre or more in height as it scrambles amongst other supporting plants.

Probably the best known, if sometimes overlooked, plant of waste places is creeping thistle (*Circium arvense*). This strong-growing perennial has the parachute seeds of the daisy family, allowing it to colonise new sites easily. It then develops a strong growing root and rhizome system, making it almost impossible to eradicate. Once established, it will spread from the wasteland habitat to meadows, garden borders, fields and even woodland margins. Its mauve flowers do attract insect pollinators and the seed heads are a firm favourite with flocks of goldfinches in late summer or early autumn.

Wasteland habitats are often short-lived themselves. Where they have been created by new development, a succession of plants will gradually move in as the ground settles, and ultimately the habitat changes to grassland or scrub, depending on the lie of the land and soil conditions. Farmland, by contrast, is usually long lasting. In the High Weald, most farmland is grazed by sheep or cattle and so is essentially grassland with a relatively poor mix of species. Tough wildflowers, such as meadow buttercup (*Ranunculus acris*) and creeping buttercup (*Ranunculus repens*) will survive the pressure of grazing. Creeping thistle is often encountered here, and clumps of nettles are frequent where cattle dung raises the nutrient level of the soil.

The tough plants that grow in these habitats are often disparaged as weeds, but they have evolved to be the first to colonise new habitats and can take advantage of mankind's waste places to find a home. Without their speedy arrival, many areas would remain barren and sterile for years until other species find them suitable for growth.

creeping buttercup

creeping thistle

CHECKLIST OF NATIVE AND NATURALISED PLANTS IN THE HIGH WEALD

The complete checklist comprises 677 taxa (including ferns and grasses). Those taxa in brown text are considered to be non-native species.

Acer campestre (field maple)
Acer platanoides (Norway maple)
Acer pseudoplatanus (sycamore)
Achillea millefolium (yarrow)
Achillea ptarmica (sneezewort)
Adoxa moschatellina (moschatel)
Aegopodium podagraria (ground elder)
Aesculus hippocastanum (horse chestnut)
Aethusa cynapium (fool's parsley)
Agrimonia eupatoria (common agrimony)
Agrimonia procera (fragrant agrimony)
Agrostis capillaris (common bent)
Agrostis stolonifera (creeping bent)
Aira caryophyllea (silver hair-grass)
Aira praecox (early hair-grass)
Ajuga reptans (bugle)
Alisma plantago-aquatica (water plantain)
Alliaria petiolata (garlic mustard)
Allium paradoxum (few-flowered garlic)
Allium triquetrum (three-cornered garlic)
Allium ursinum (ramsons)
Allium vineale (wild onion)
Alnus glutinosa (alder)
Alopecurus geniculatus (marsh foxtail)
Alopecurus myosuroides (black-grass)
Alopecurus pratensis (meadow foxtail)
Althaea hirsuta (rough marsh mallow)
Althaea officinalis (marsh mallow)
Anacamptis morio (green winged orchid)
Anacamptis pyramidalis (pyramidal orchid)
Anagallis arvensis (scarlet pimpernel)
Anagallis tenella (bog pimpernel)
Anemone nemorosa (wood anemone)
Angelica sylvestris (wild angelica)
Anisantha sterilis (barren brome)
Anthoxanthum odoratum (sweet vernal grass)
Anthriscus caucalis (bur chervil)
Anthriscus sylvestris (cow parsley)
Aphanes arvensis (parsley piert)

Apium graveolens (wild celery)
Apium nodiflorum (fool's water-cress)
Aquilegia vulgaris (columbine)
Arabidopsis thaliana (thale cress)
Arctium lappa (great burdock)
Arctium minus (lesser burdock)
Arenaria serpyllifolia (thyme-leaved sandwort)
Armeria maritima (thrift)
Arrhenantherum elatius (false oat-grass)
Artemisia cotula (stinking chamomile)
Artemisia maritima (sea wormwood)
Artemisia vulgaris (mugwort)
Arum italicum (Italian lords and ladies)
Arum maculatum (lords and ladies or cuckoo-pint)
Asplenium adiantum-nigrum (black spleenwort)
Asplenium ruta-muraria (wall-rue)
Asplenium scolopendrium (hart's-tongue fern)
Asplenium trichomanes (maidenhair spleenwort)
Aster tripolium (sea aster)
Athyrium filix-femina (lady fern)
Atriplex patula (common orache)
Atriplex prostrata (spur-leaved orache)
Ballota nigra (black horehound)
Barbarea intermedia (medium-flowered winter cress)
Barbarea vulgaris (common yellow rocket or winter cress)
Bellis perennis (common daisy)
Betula pendula (silver birch)
Betula pubescens (downy birch)
Bidens cernua (nodding bur-marigold)
Bistorta amplexicaulis (red bistort)
Blechnum spicant (hard fern)
Bolboschoenus maritimus (sea club-rush)
Brachypodium sylvaticum (false brome)
Briza media (quaking grass)
Bromus erectus (upright brome)
Bromus ramosus (hairy brome)
Bryonia dioica (white bryony)
Bupleurum tenuissimum (slender hare's-ear)
Butomus umbellatus (flowering rush)

Buxus sempervirens (box)
Cakile maritima (sea rocket)
Callitriche hamulata (intermediate water starwort)
Callitriche obtusangula (blunt-fruited water starwort)
Callitriche platycarpa (various-leaved water starwort)
Callitriche stagnalis (common water starwort)
Calluna vulgaris (ling or heather)
Caltha palustris (marsh marigold)
Calystegia sepium (hedge bindweed)
Calystegia silvatica (large bindweed)
Calystegia soldanella (sea bindweed)
Campanula rotundifolia (harebell)
Capsella bursa-pastoris (shepherd's purse)
Cardamine amara (large bitter cress)
Cardamine flexuosa (wavy bitter cress)
Cardamine hirsuta (hairy bitter cress)
Cardamine pratensis (lady's smock or cuckoo flower)
Carduus crispus (welted thistle)
Carduus tenuiflorus (slender thistle)
Carex acutiformis (lesser pond sedge)
Carex binervis (green-ribbed sedge)
Carex caryophyllea (spring sedge)
Carex curta (white sedge)
Carex demissa (yellow sedge)
Carex distans (distant sedge)
Carex divulsa (grey sedge)
Carex echinata (star sedge)
Carex flacca (glaucous sedge)
Carex hirta (hairy sedge)
Carex laevigata (smooth-stalked sedge)
Carex leporina (oval sedge)
Carex muricata (prickly sedge)
Carex nigra (common sedge)
Carex otrubae (false fox-sedge)
Carex pallescens (pale sedge)
Carex panicea (carnation sedge)
Carex paniculata (greater tussock sedge)
Carex pendula (pendulous sedge)
Carex pilulifera (pill sedge)
Carex pseudocyperus (cyperus sedge)
Carex pulicaris (flea sedge)
Carex remota (remote sedge)
Carex riparia (greater pond sedge)
Carex spicata (spiked sedge)
Carex strigosa (thin-spiked wood sedge)
Carex sylvatica (wood sedge)
Carex vesicaria (bladder sedge)
Carpinus betulus (hornbeam)
Castanea sativa (sweet chestnut)
Centaurea nigra (common knapweed)

Centaurium erythraea (common centaury)
Centaurium pulchellum (lesser centaury)
Centranthus ruber (red valerian)
Centunculus minimus (chaffweed)
Cerastium arvense (field mouse-ear)
Cerastium diffusum (sea mouse-ear)
Cerastium fontanum (common mouse-ear)
Cerastium glomeratum (clustered mouse-ear)
Ceratocapnos claviculata (climbing corydalis)
Ceratophyllum demersum (rigid hornwort)
Ceratophyllum submersum (soft hornwort)
Ceterach officinarum (rustyback fern)
Chamaemelum nobile (chamomile)
Chamerion angustifolium (rosebay willowherb)
Cheiranthus cheiri (wallflower)
Chelidonium majus (greater celandine)
Chenopodium album (fat hen)
Chenopodium polyspermum (many-seeded goosefoot)
Chrysosplenium oppositifolium (opposite-leaved golden saxifrage)
Cicendia filiformis (yellow centaury)
Circaea lutetiana (enchanter's nightshade)
Cirsium arvense (creeping thistle)
Cirsium dissectum (meadow thistle)
Cirsium palustre (marsh thistle)
Cirsium vulgare (spear thistle)
Claytonia sibirica (pink purslane)
Clematis vitalba (old man's beard)
Clinopodium vulgare (wild basil)
Cochlearia danica (Danish scurvygrass)
Conium maculatum (hemlock)
Conopodium majus (pignut)
Convallaria majalis (lily of the valley)
Convolvulus arvensis (field bindweed)
Cornus sanguinea (dogwood)
Corylus avellana (hazel)
Crambe maritima (sea kale)
Crassula helmsii (New Zealand pygmyweed)
Crataegus laevigata (midland hawthorn)
Crataegus monogyna (hawthorn)
Crataegus × media (hybrid hawthorn)
Crepis capillaris (smooth hawk's-beard)
Crepis vesicaria (beaked hawk's-beard)
Crithmum maritimum (rock samphire)
Cruciata laevipes (crosswort)
Cuscuta epithymum (dodder)
Cymbalaria muralis (ivy-leaved toadflax)
Cynoglossum officinale (hound's tongue)
Cynosurus cristatus (crested dog's tail)
Cytisus scoparius (broom)

Dactylis glomerata (cock's foot)
Dactylorhiza fuchsii (common spotted orchid)
Dactylorhiza incarnata (early marsh orchid)
Dactylorhiza maculata (heath spotted orchid)
Dactylorhiza praetermissa (southern marsh orchid)
Danthonia decumbens (heath grass)
Daphne laureola (spurge laurel)
Daucus carota (wild carrot)
Deschampsia cespitosa (tufted hair-grass)
Deschampsia flexuosa (wavy hair-grass)
Digitalis purpurea (foxglove)
Dioscorea communis (black bryony)
Dipsacus fullonum (teasel)
Drosera intermedia (oblong-leaved sundew)
Drosera rotundifolia (round-leaved sundew)
Dryopteris aemula (hay-scented buckler fern)
Dryopteris affinis (scaly male fern)
Dryopteris carthusiana (narrow buckler fern)
Dryopteris dilatata (broad buckler fern)
Dryopteris filix-mas (male fern)
Echium vulgare (viper's bugloss)
Eleocharis multicaulis (many-stalked spike-rush)
Eleocharis palustris (common spike-rush)
Elodea canadensis (Canadian waterweed)
Elodea nuttallii (Nutall's waterweed)
Elymus caninus (bearded couch)
Elymus pycnanthus (sea couch)
Elytrigia repens (common couch)
Epilobium brunnescens (New Zealand willowherb)
Epilobium ciliatum (American willowherb)
Epilobium hirsutum (great willowherb)
Epilobium lanceolatum (spur-leaved willowherb)
Epilobium montanum (broad-leaved willowherb)
Epilobium obscurum (short-fruited willowherb)
Epilobium palustre (marsh willowherb)
Epilobium parviflorum (hairy willowherb)
Epilobium roseum (pale willowherb)
Epilobium tetragonum (square-stalked willowherb)
Epipactis helleborine (broad-leaved helleborine)
Epipactis purpurata (violet helleborine)
Equisetum arvense (field horsetail)
Equisetum fluviatile (water horsetail)
Equisetum palustre (marsh horsetail)
Equisetum telmateia (great horsetail)
Erica cinerea (bell heather)
Erica tetralix (cross-leaved heath)
Erigeron canadensis (Canadian fleabane)
Eriophorum angustifolium (common cotton grass)
Erodium cicutarium (common stork's-bill)
Erophila verna (common whitlowgrass)
Eryngium maritimum (sea holly)

Erysimum cheiranthoides (treacle mustard)
Euonymus europaeus (spindle)
Eupatorium cannabinum (hemp agrimony)
Euphorbia amygdaloides (wood spurge)
Euphorbia helioscopia (sun spurge)
Euphorbia peplus (petty spurge)
Euphrasia officinalis (eyebright)
Fagus sylvatica (beech)
Fallopia japonica (Japanese knotweed)
Festuca arundinacea (tall fescue)
Festuca gigantea (giant fescue)
Festuca ovina (sheep's fescue)
Festuca pratensis (meadow fescue)
Festuca rubra (red fescue)
Ficaria verna (lesser celandine)
Filago minima (least cudweed)
Filipendula ulmaria (meadowsweet)
Fragaria vesca (wild strawberry)
Frangula alnus (alder buckthorn)
Frankenia laevis (sea heath)
Fraxinus excelsior (ash)
Fumaria officinalis (common fumitory)
Galanthus nivalis (snowdrop)
Galega officinalis (goat's rue)
Galeopsis angustifolia (red hemp-nettle)
Galeopsis tetrahit (common hemp-nettle)
Galium aparine (cleavers or goosegrass)
Galium mollugo (hedge bedstraw)
Galium odoratum (sweet woodruff)
Galium palustre (marsh bedstraw)
Galium saxatile (heath bedstraw)
Galium uliginosum (fen bedstraw)
Galium verum (lady's bedstraw)
Genista anglica (petty whin)
Genista pilosa (hairy greenweed)
Genista tinctoria (Dyer's greenweed)
Gentiana pneumonanthe (marsh gentian)
Geranium dissectum (cut-leaved cranesbill)
Geranium molle (dove's-foot cranesbill)
Geranium robertianum (herb Robert)
Geum urbanum (wood avens)
Glaucium flavum (horned yellow poppy)
Glechoma hederacea (ground ivy)
Glyceria declinata (small sweet-grass)
Glyceria fluitans (floating sweet-grass)
Glyceria maxima (reed sweet-grass)
Glyceria notata (plicate sweet-grass)
Gnaphalium sylvaticum (wood cudweed)
Gnaphalium uliginosum (marsh cudweed)
Gymnadenia conopsea (fragrant orchid)
Halimione portulacoides (sea purslane)

Hedera helix (common ivy)

Helictotrichon pubescens (downy oat-grass)

Helminthotheca echioides (bristly ox-tongue)

Heracleum mantegazzianum (giant hogweed)

Heracleum sphondylium (hogweed)

Hieracium lachenalii subsp. *argillaceum* (southern hawkweed)

Hieracium sabaudum (autumn hawkweed)

Hieracium trichocaulon (hairy-stemmed hawkweed)

Hieracium umbellatum (umbellate hawkweed)

Holcus lanatus (Yorkshire fog)

Holcus mollis (creeping soft-grass)

Honckenya peploides (sea sandwort)

Hordeum marinum (sea barley)

Hordeum murinum (wall barley)

Hordeum secalinum (meadow barley)

Humulus lupulus (hop)

Hyacinthoides hispanica (Spanish bluebell)

Hyacinthoides × *massartiana* (hybrid bluebell)

Hyacinthoides non-scripta (English bluebell)

Hydrocotyle vulgaris (marsh pennywort)

Hymenophyllum tunbrigense (Tunbridge filmy fern)

Hyoscyamus niger (henbane)

Hypericum androsaemum (tutsan)

Hypericum calycinum (rose of Sharon)

Hypericum elodes (marsh St John's wort)

Hypericum humifusum (creeping St John's wort)

Hypericum maculatum (imperforate St John's wort)

Hypericum perforatum (perforate St John's wort)

Hypericum pulchrum (beautiful St John's wort)

Hypericum tetrapterum (square-stalked St John's wort)

Hypochaeris radicata (cat's-ear)

Ilex aquifolium (holly)

Impatiens glandulifera (Himalayan balsam)

Impatiens parviflora (small balsam)

Iris foetidissima (stinking iris)

Iris pseudacorus (yellow iris)

Isolepis fluitans (floating spike-rush)

Isolepis setacea (bristle club-rush)

Jacobaea vulgaris (ragwort)

Juncus acutiflorus (sharp-flowered rush)

Juncus articulatus (jointed rush)

Juncus bufonius (toad rush)

Juncus bulbosus (bulbous rush)

Juncus conglomeratus (compact rush)

Juncus effusus (soft rush)

Juncus gerardii (saltmarsh rush)

Juncus inflexus (hard rush)

Juncus squarrosus (heath rush)

Juncus tenuis (slender rush)

Kickxia elatine (sharp-leaved fluellin)

Lactuca muralis (wall lettuce)

Lactuca serriola (prickly lettuce)

Lagarosiphon major (curly waterweed)

Lamium album (white dead-nettle)

Lamium galeobdolon (yellow archangel)

Lamium purpureum (red dead-nettle)

Lapsana communis (nipple-wort)

Lathraea clandestina (purple toothwort)

Lathyrus japonicus subsp. *maritimus* (sea pea)

Lathyrus linifolius (bitter vetch)

Lathyrus nissolia (grass-leaved vetchling)

Lathyrus pratensis (meadow pea)

Lemna minor (common duckweed)

Lemna minuta (least duckweed)

Lemna trisulca (ivy-leaved duckweed)

Leontodon hispidus (rough hawkbit)

Leontodon saxatilis (lesser hawkbit)

Lepidium coronopus (swine cress)

Lepidium didymum (lesser swine cress)

Leucanthemum vulgare (ox-eye daisy)

Ligustrum vulgare (privet)

Littorella uniflora (shoreweed)

Linaria purpurea (purple toadflax)

Linaria vulgaris (common toadflax)

Linum catharticum (fairy flax)

Lolium perenne (perennial rye-grass)

Lonicera periclymenum (honeysuckle)

Lotus corniculatus (bird's foot trefoil)

Lotus pedunculatus (marsh bird's foot trefoil)

Lunaria annua (honesty)

Luzula campestris (field wood rush)

Luzula forsteri (southern wood rush)

Luzula multiflora (heath wood rush)

Luzula pilosa (hairy wood rush)

Luzula sylvatica (great wood rush)

Lycium barbarum (Duke of Argyll's tea tree)

Lycopodiella inundata (marsh clubmoss)

Lycopodium clavatum (stag's-horn clubmoss)

Lycopus europaeus (gypsywort)

Lysichiton americanus (skunk cabbage)

Lysimachia maritima (sea milkwort)

Lysimachia nemorum (yellow pimpernel)

Lysimachia nummularia (creeping Jenny)

Lythrum portula (water purslane)

Lythrum salicaria (purple loosestrife)

Malus pumila (apple)

Malus sylvestris (crab apple)

Malva moschata (musk mallow)

Malva sylvestris (common mallow)

Matricaria chamomilla (scented mayweed)
Matricaria discoidea (pineapple weed)
Medicago arabica (spotted medic)
Medicago lupulina (black medic)
Medicago polymorpha (toothed medic)
Medicago sativa (lucerne)
Melampyrum pratense (common cow-wheat)
Melica uniflora (wood melick)
Mentha aquatica (water mint)
Mentha arvensis (corn mint)
Mentha × verticillata (whorled mint)
Menyanthes trifoliata (bogbean)
Mercurialis annua (annual mercury)
Mercurialis perennis (dog's mercury)
Milium effusum (wood millet)
Mimulus guttatus (monkeyflower)
Moehringia trinervia (three-nerved sandwort)
Moenchia erecta (upright chickweed)
Molina caerulea (purple moor grass)
Montia fontana (blinks)
Myosotis arvensis (common forget-me-not)
Myosotis discolor (changing forget-me-not)
Myosotis laxa (tufted forget-me-not)
Myosotis ramosissima (early forget-me-not)
Myosotis scorpioides (water forget-me-not)
Myosotis secunda (creeping forget-me-not)
Myosotis sylvatica (wood forget-me-not)
Myosoton aquaticum (water chickweed)
Myosurus minimus (mousetail)
Myriophyllum alternifolium (alternate water milfoil)
Myriophyllum spicatum (spiked water milfoil)
Narcissus pseudonarcissus (wild daffodil)
Nardus stricta (mat grass)
Narthecium ossifragum (bog asphodel)
Nasturtium officinale (watercress)
Neottia nidus-avis (bird's nest orchid)
Neottia ovata (twayblade)
Nuphar lutea (brandy bottle or yellow waterlily)
Nymphaea alba (white waterlily)
Odontites vernus (red bartsia)
Oenanthe crocata (hemlock water dropwort)
Oenanthe fistulosa (tubular water dropwort)
Oenanthe lachenalii (parsley water dropwort)
Oenothera glazioviana (large-flowered evening primrose)
Onoclea sensibilis (sensitive fern)
Ophioglossum vulgatum (adder's tongue fern)
Orchis mascula (early purple orchid)
Oreopteris limbosperma (lemon-scented fern)
Origanum vulgare (marjoram)
Ornithopus perpusillus (bird's-foot)
Orobanche minor (lesser broomrape)

Orobanche rapum-genistae (great broomrape)
Osmunda regalis (royal fern)
Oxalis acetosella (wood sorrel)
Oxalis corniculata (procumbent yellow-sorrel)
Oxalis debilis (large-flowered pink wood-sorrel)
Oxalis stricta (upright yellow-sorrel)
Pedicularis sylvatica (lousewort)
Persicaria amphibia (amphibious bistort)
Persicaria bistorta (bistort)
Persicaria hydropiper (water pepper)
Persicaria lapathifolia (pale persicaria)
Persicaria maculosa (redshank)
Persicaria wallichii (Himalayan knotweed)
Petasites fragrans (winter heliotrope)
Petasites hybridus (butterbur)
Petasites japonicus (giant butterbur)
Phegopteris connectilis (beech fern)
Phleum bertolonii (smaller cat's tail)
Phleum pratense (Timothy grass)
Phragmites australis (common reed)
Pilosella officinarum (mouse-ear hawkweed)
Pimpinella saxifraga (burnet saxifrage)
Pinus sylvestris (Scots pine)
Plantago coronopus (buck's-horn plantain)
Plantago lanceolata (ribwort plantain)
Plantago major (great plantain)
Plantago maritima (sea plantain)
Plantago media (hoary plantain)
Platanthera chlorantha (butterfly orchid)
Poa annua (annual meadow grass)
Poa bulbosa (bulbous meadow grass)
Poa nemoralis (wood meadow grass)
Poa pratensis (smooth meadow grass)
Poa trivialis (rough meadow grass)
Polygala serpyllifolia (heath milkwort)
Polygala vulgaris (common milkwort)
Polygonum arenastrum (equal-leaved knotgrass)
Polygonum aviculare (knotgrass)
Polypodium vulgare (common polypody)
Polystichum aculeatum (hard shield fern)
Polystichum setiferum (soft shield fern)
Populus alba (white poplar)
Populus tremula (aspen)
Potamogeton berchtoldii (small pondweed)
Potamogeton natans (broad-leaved pondweed)
Potamogeton polygonifolius (bog pondweed)
Potamogeton pusillus (lesser pondweed)
Potentilla anglica (creeping tormentil)
Potentilla anserina (silverweed)
Potentilla erecta (tormentil)
Potentilla reptans (cinquefoil)

Potentilla sterilis (barren strawberry)
Primula × polyantha (false oxlip)
Primula veris (cowslip)
Primula vulgaris (primrose)
Prunella vulgaris (self-heal)
Prunus avium (wild cherry)
Prunus cerasifera (cherry plum)
Prunus domestica (plum)
Prunus laurocerasus (cherry laurel)
Prunus spinosa (blackthorn)
Pseudofumaria lutea (yellow corydalis)
Pteridium aquilinum (bracken)
Puccinellia distans (reflexed saltmarsh grass)
Puccinellia maritima (common saltmarsh grass)
Pulicaria dysenterica (common fleabane)
Quercus cerris (Turkey oak)
Quercus petraea (sessile oak)
Quercus robur (pedunculate or common oak)
Radiola linoides (allseed)
Ranunculus acris (meadow buttercup)
Ranunculus bulbosus (bulbous buttercup)
Ranunculus flammula (lesser spearwort)
Ranunculus lingua (greater spearwort)
Ranunculus omiophyllus (round-leaved crowfoot)
Ranunculus peltatus (pond water-crowfoot)
Ranunculus repens (creeping buttercup)
Ranunculus sardous (hairy buttercup)
Ranunculus sceleratus (celery-leaved buttercup)
Reseda lutea (greenweed or wild mignonette)
Rhinanthus minor (yellow rattle)
Rhododendron ponticum (rhododendron)
Rhynchospora alba (white beak-sedge)
Ribes nigrum (black currant)
Ribes rubrum (red currant)
Ribes sanguineum (flowering currant)
Ribes uva-crispa (gooseberry)
Rosa arvensis (field rose)
Rosa canina (dog rose)
Rosa micrantha (small-flowered sweet briar)
Rosa rubiginosa (sweet briar)
Rosa stylosa (short-styled rose)
Rosa tomentosa (harsh downy-rose)
Rubus caesius (dewberry)
Rubus fruticosus (bramble)
Rubus idaeus (raspberry)
Rumex acetosa (common sorrel)
Rumex acetosella (sheep's sorrel)
Rumex conglomeratus (clustered dock)
Rumex crispus (curled dock)
Rumex obtusifolius (broad-leaved dock)
Rumex sanguineus (wood dock)

Ruscus aculeatus (butcher's broom)
Sagina apetala (annual pearlwort)
Sagina apetala subsp. *erecta* (annual pearlwort)
Sagina procumbens (procumbent pearlwort)
Sagittaria sagittifolia (arrowhead)
Salix atrocinerea (grey willow)
Salix aurita (eared willow)
Salix caprea (goat willow)
Salix fragilis (crack willow)
Salix repens (creeping willow)
Salvia verbenaca (wild clary)
Sambucus nigra (elderberry)
Samolus valerandi (brookweed)
Sanicula europaea (sanicle)
Saxifraga tridactylites (rue-leaved saxifrage)
Scirpus sylvaticus (wood club-rush)
Scorzoneroides autumnalis (autumn hawkbit)
Scrophularia auriculata (water figwort)
Scrophularia nodosa (figwort)
Scutellaria galericulata (skullcap)
Scutellaria minor (lesser skullcap)
Scutellaria × nicholsonii (hybrid skullcap)
Sedum acre (biting stonecrop)
Sedum album (white stonecrop)
Sedum anglicum (English stonecrop)
Sedum telephium (orpine)
Senecio aquaticus (marsh ragwort)
Senecio erucifolius (hoary ragwort)
Senecio squalidus (Oxford ragwort)
Senecio sylvaticus (heath groundsel)
Senecio viscosus (sticky groundsel)
Senecio vulgaris (groundsel)
Serratula tinctoria (saw-wort)
Sherardia arvensis (madder)
Sibthorpia europaea (Cornish moneywort)
Silaum silaus (pepper saxifrage)
Silene dioica (red campion)
Silene flos-cuculi (ragged robin)
Silene latifolia (white campion)
Silene uniflora (sea campion)
Silene vulgaris (bladder campion)
Sinapis arvensis (charlock)
Sisymbrium officinale (hedge mustard)
Smyrnium olusatrum (alexanders)
Solanum dulcamara (woody nightshade or bittersweet)
Solanum nigrum (black nightshade)
Solidago gigantea (early goldenrod)
Solidago virgaurea (goldenrod)
Sonchus arvensis (corn sowthistle)
Sonchus asper (prickly sowthistle)
Sonchus oleraceus (common sowthistle)

Sorbus aria (whitebeam)
Sorbus aucuparia (rowan or mountain ash)
Sorbus torminalis (wild service tree)
Sparganium emersum (unbranched bur-reed)
Sparganium erectum (branched bur-reed)
Spergula arvensis (corn spurrey)
Spergularia marina (lesser sea-spurrey)
Spergularia media (greater sea-spurrey)
Spergularia rubra (sand spurrey)
Spiranthes spiralis (autumn lady's tresses)
Stachys arvensis (field woundwort)
Stachys officinalis (betony)
Stachys palustris (marsh woundwort)
Stachys sylvatica (wood woundwort)
Stellaria graminea (lesser stitchwort)
Stellaria holostea (greater stitchwort)
Stellaria media (chickweed)
Stellaria uliginosa (bog stitchwort)
Stratiotes aloides (water soldier)
Stuckenia pectinata (fennel pondweed)
Suaeda maritima (annual sea blite)
Succisa pratensis (devil's bit scabious)
Symphytum officinale (comfrey)
Symphytum tuberosum (tuberous comfrey)
Symphytum × uplandicum (Russian comfrey)
Tanacetum parthenium (feverfew)
Tanacetum vulgare (tansy)
Taraxacum officinale (dandelion)
Taxus baccata (yew)
Teucrium scorodonia (wood sage)
Thelypteris palustris (marsh fern)
Thymus praecox subsp. *polytrichus* (wild thyme)
Thymus pulegioides (large thyme)
Tilia cordata (small-leaved lime)
Tilia × europaea (lime)
Torilis japonica (hedge parsley)
Torilis nodosa (knotted hedge parlsey)
Tragopogon pratensis (goat's beard)
Trichophorum cespitosum (deer grass)
Trifolium arvense (hare's-foot clover)
Trifolium campestre (hop trefoil)
Trifolium dubium (lesser trefoil)
Trifolium hybridum (alsike clover)
Trifolium medium (zigzag clover)
Trifolium micranthum (slender trefoil)
Trifolium pratense (red clover)
Trifolium repens (white clover)
Trifolium striatum (knotted clover)
Triglochin maritima (sea arrowgrass)

Triglochin palustris (marsh arrowgrass)
Tripleurospermum inodorum (scentless mayweed)
Trisetum flavescens (yellow oat-grass)
Tussilago farfara (coltsfoot)
Typha angustifolia (lesser bulrush)
Typha latifolia (bulrush)
Ulex europaeus (gorse)
Ulex minor (dwarf gorse)
Ulmus glabra (wych elm)
Ulmus minor (English elm)
Urtica dioica (stinging nettle)
Urtica urens (small nettle)
Vaccinium myrtillus (bilberry)
Vaccinium oxycoccus (cranberry)
Valeriana dioica (marsh valerian)
Valeriana officinalis (valerian)
Valerianella carinata (keel-fruited cornsalad)
Verbascum blattaria (moth mullein)
Verbascum thapsus (great mullein)
Veronica agrestis (green field-speedwell)
Veronica arvensis (wall speedwell)
Veronica beccabunga (brooklime)
Veronica chamaedrys (germander speedwell)
Veronica filiformis (slender speedwell)
Veronica hederifolia subsp. *hederifolia* (ivy-leaved speedwell)
Veronica hederifolia subsp. *lucorum* (ivy-leaved speedwell)
Veronica montana (wood speedwell)
Veronica officinalis (common speedwell)
Veronica peregrina (American speedwell)
Veronica persica (Persian field-speedwell)
Veronica polita (grey field-speedwell)
Veronica scutellata (marsh speedwell)
Veronica serpyllifolia (thyme-leaved speedwell)
Viburnum opulus (guelder rose)
Vicia cracca (tufted vetch)
Vicia hirsuta (hairy tare)
Vicia sativa subsp. *nigra* (narrow-leaved vetch)
Vicia sativa subsp. *segetalis* (common vetch)
Vicia sepium (bush vetch)
Vicia tetrasperma (smooth tare)
Viola arvensis (field pansy)
Viola canina (heath dog violet)
Viola odorata (sweet violet)
Viola palustris (marsh violet)
Viola reichenbachiana (early dog violet)
Viola riviniana (common dog violet)
Vulpia bromoides (squirrel-tail fescue)
Wahlenbergia hederacea (ivy-leaved bellflower)

CONSERVING THE FUTURE

Throughout the High Weald, careful management of the many varied habitats is helping to maintain and increase the local biodiversity, but plant species around the world are under threat. As a result, around a quarter of the world's plant species — between 60,000 and 100,000 species — face possible extinction.

At Wakehurst, the Millennium Seed Bank (MSB) works with partners in more than 80 countries to bank seeds of the world's wild plant species, focusing on plants that are most at risk and most useful for the future. At the MSB's striking facilities, scientists work on seed banking theory and technology. They have already secured over 13% of the world's wild plant species in the MSB and in partner seed banks around the world. By 2020, their aim is to have safely stored seed from 25% of the world's bankable plants and to include within this number all of our native wildflowers and trees.

Not that this apparently simple task is easily completed. Seeds come in all shapes and sizes and, depending on the environment in which they have evolved, they require particular conditions for long-term storage. Some, like the English oak, remain a riddle, but most can survive for hundreds of years if they are dried and then stored at -20°C. MSB scientists not only develop protocols for the optimisation of storage conditions for each species, but they also investigate how to break dormancy. This 'wakes' the seeds up again, so that they germinate and grow into a new plants when the time is right.

Downland display bed at
the Millennium Seed Bank

For our native wildflowers, the UK Native Seed Hub project aims to make high-quality seed available for use in conservation and restoration. 98% of the semi-natural grassland once present in England and Wales has vanished since the 1930s, so this project began by growing lowland meadow species. Seed-production beds multiply collections of priority species, such as devil's bit scabious (*Succisa pratensis*), cuckoo flower (*Cardamine pratensis*), green field-speedwell (*Veronica agrestis*), spiked rampion (*Phyteuma spicatum*) and harebell (*Campanula rotundifolia*). The project provides seed and plug-grown plantlets for direct use in habitat restoration. Underpinned by Kew's world-class botanical, horticultural, ecological and seed conservation expertise, the project offers training, technical advice and research to landowners and agencies.

spiked rampion

ACKNOWLEDGEMENTS

The author would like to acknowledge the following for their help and advice: Gina Fullerlove, Georgina Hills and Sharon Whitehead. Thanks also to Christine Beard for typesetting and layout design. Finally, thanks to Arthur Hoare for his immense help with the scope and content of this book. Arthur's advice was invaluable in ensuring the completed book is worthy of the initial concept — an accessible guide to wildflowers for visitors and residents of the High Weald.

FURTHER INFORMATION

The High Weald Area of Outstanding Beauty Unit can provide detailed help and advice. Their unit is based in Flimwell:
High Weald AONB Unit, Woodland Enterprise Centre, Hastings Road, Flimwell, East Sussex TN5 7PR
info@highweald.org

For a comprehensive guide to the flowers of Sussex, *The Flora of Sussex*, published in 2018 by the Sussex Botanical Recording Society, provides an unparalleled volume:
Sussex Botanical Recording Society (2018). *The Flora of Sussex*. Nature Bureau.

common spotted orchid

INDEX TO COMMON NAMES

Images are indicated by page numbers in **bold**.

monkeyflower

INDEX TO SCIENTIFIC NAMES